We had just finished supper in the maximum security section of San Quentin Prison. As we were returning to our cells, someone shouted "fire," and several guards ran toward flames on the first tier; they did not realize that it was only a diversionary strategy designed to clear one end of the cell block.

As soon as the guards were out of the area, several inmates rushed up to one convict on the second tier. He was standing with his hands in his pockets, but as he saw his attackers coming, he tried to ward off their assault. There was little he could do. The knife penetrated deep into his stomach. He exhaled sharply, weakly lifting his right hand to make the sign of the cross before he fell in a heap, the life gone from his body.

As I was soon to find out, murder was an accepted part of life in San Quentin Prison.

San Quentin and Beyond

by Larry O. Howland

Whitaker House
504 LAUREL DRIVE, MONROEVILLE, PA 15146

ISBN: 0-88368-050-5
© 1974 by Whitaker House
Printed in the United States of America

*Some of the names in this book have been changed to protect the
individuals involved.*

Whitaker House
504 LAUREL DRIVE MONROEVILLE PA 15146

Dedicated to
Bonnie, my faithful wife,
Rebecca, my loving daughter,
Pastor E.W. Zuber,
and
Wesley Smith

Table of Contents

Foreword

San Quentin and Beyond is the kind of book I couldn't put down. The exciting story on these pages reaches out and pulls the reader into the emotion of every event.

I appreciated this book so much because I know the author behind it. His life has been dramatically changed by Jesus Christ; and he has continued to move into the kind of Christian maturity that brings honor and glory to the Lord.

When Larry met Christ he was a high school drop-out and a criminal. Jesus started such a revolution in his life that Larry is now a college graduate, with honors, and has received his master's degree.

But more than the education is the real story, the real Larry, the Larry you will meet in this book, what he was, and what he now is in Christ.

The great challenge of these pages is not only that God can change a life once shipwrecked and ruined, but that He can take that life off the sandbar of decay and use it as an effective rescue vessel for others.

Wesley E. Smith
Full Life Crusade
Boynton Beach, Fla.

Introduction

Murder is the routine of life in San Quentin. In writing of prisons in the October, 1974, issue of *Reader's Digest*, Nathan M. Adams declares that San Quentin is the most violent prison in our country. He states that in 1973 there were fifty-four convicts stabbed.

It is not a pleasant place to be, but it was my home for almost two years. I'm inviting you to join me there as I share my story. It is the story of a wrecked life, and of a God who cares—not only for those in the sanctuary on Sunday morning, but also for those who are seemingly beyond the reach of God.

> Larry O. Howland
> P.O. Box 363
> Elsie, Michigan 48831

Chapter
1

Like Father, Like Son

It was a lousy place for a brawl.

The little French village looked just like a Christmas display—the kind they used to put in the windows of department stores back in the States. Even though it was the middle of January it seemed there ought to be a Salvation Army lassie ringing her bell, and a P.A. system belching, "Santa Claus is Coming to Town."

It was dark, and the cobblestone street was almost empty. The few people on the sidewalk seemed to be headed for the bakery. The bakery was going full blast, and the crisp night air was sweet with the yeasty fragrance of bread, fresh from the ovens. Several people were sitting at tiny· tables in the little cake-and-coffee shop that was part of the bakery, and we could see them through the window as our Simca rolled into town.

There were only a few people on the narrow street —one a heavy-set French girl with a round face sticking out from a sky-blue kerchief; the other, a frail-looking workman carrying a long loaf of fresh bread.

We were drunk, all four of us G.I.'s—John Morton, Darrell Stockwell, John Eason and myself. When we were right in front of the bakery, John Morton rolled down his window and whistled at the girl. Then he yelled at her and waved his arm.

The frog with the loaf of bread shook his fist at us, shouting something in fast French.

John Morton is a former Golden Gloves boxer, 245 pounds, all muscle. He was the only one of the four who got really mean when he was drunk. When alcohol hit his bloodstream it seemed to switch off his brain and turn him into a windmill. All he wanted to do was fight.

John yelled at me to stop the car, so I slammed on the brakes, skidding sideways on the snow-covered cobbles. Now there was going to be some action!

John jumped out of the back seat and took a swing at the frog with his big, heavy fist. The road was icy, and John slipped, sliding right past the guy.

The frog dropped the loaf of bread and walloped John on the back of the neck. Down he went, cursing like crazy.

I wasn't generally pugnacious, but I was as tanked as the rest of them, and I wasn't about to see my buddy—a Golden Gloves boxer, at that—clobbered by this little guy. I punched him in the stomach. The Frenchman clutched at his stomach and started to run, slipping and sliding on the smooth cobblestones. Darrell, John Eason and I took after him while John Morton pulled himself together.

All four of us were chasing this little guy when he slipped and fell. He seemed to twist as he went down, and then he doubled up with pain. When he saw us bearing down on him, he covered his head with his arms.

Kicking at him and punching him was like kicking and hitting a little kid. He was such a little guy. He tried to get up, and when he got his head and shoulders off the street I kicked at him again with my heavy boot. He screamed

14

and clutched his chest, his eyes wide with pain and terror.

I was about to put my boot in his face when somebody tugged at my jacket. I turned to see a big, middle-aged woman with a string bag full of bread, shaking her finger at me. She was jabbering at me in furious French, but when she saw that I didn't understand everything, she tried English.

"Stop! Pig! American pig! Stop! I call gendarme!" she cried, all the time shaking her finger and glaring at me.

"Man, let's beat it!" John Eason shouted, and we all scrambled into the Simca.

I switched the motor on. The wheels spun against the slippery cobblestones. I cursed. My head was clearing now. I realized what we had done, and I felt sick from sudden disgust. As I told you, I wasn't generally a pugnacious person; I wouldn't ever have hurt that little guy when I was sober.

However, my compassion for the injured frog quickly faded, erased by my fear of getting caught. The police would be coming in a matter of minutes, and I sure didn't want to tangle with the French cops.

The ice melted under the spinning tires, and we jerked away from the curb, fish-tailing down the narrow road, leaving the little Christmas village and heading back to our army base at Fontainebleau.

Two weeks later, at the end of January 1963, I found myself on trial before a military court for the third time within a year.

A dour-looking colonel who was the presiding officer called me to stand at attention before him while he read my sentence. Even though it was January, I suddenly felt very hot and uncomfortable. For one fleeting moment, I considered turning my back and walking out of the room. The olive drab color of the walls seemed to symbolize the army authority, which I despised and rebelled against. For a change of scenery, I looked up at the white ceiling as the colonel cleared his throat and prepared to read.

"You are hereby reduced from the rank of Specialist Fourth Class to the rank of Private E-1. You are to be restricted to base for a period of sixty days and will also forfeit one-half of your next three months' pay."

I wanted to tell him what he could do with my pay and with the whole army. I hated this place and only wanted out. The colonel continued speaking, his voice a monotone, and his eyes seemingly riveted to the paper he held in his hand.

"Private Howland, this court feels a responsibility to inform you that you have been a disgrace to your unit and to your fellow soldiers . . . ."

His voice droned on and on, but my ears shut out his words. I suddenly pictured him with an apple in his mouth, roasting over a very hot fire. It was a humorous picture, and I had to suppress the beginnings of a smile. As he continued his lecture, I thought of the many lectures I had received from my mother before I joined the army.

"You're going to turn out just like your father." I could almost hear the familiar words. While he was in the army, my father had been convicted of murdering another soldier and consequently had been given a dishonorable discharge. I had been told that my father had also been involved in a bank robbery, for which he was never apprehended. And now here I was, undergoing my third court martial and, like my father, facing a discharge—one that would rid the army of a rebellious soldier full of hatred. I pondered my hatred and rebellion, trying to think when they had first begun. It seemed they had been a part of me for as long as I could remember.

As the colonel continued to read, my mind went back to the pleasant suburban street in Fairborn, Ohio. It was 1947, and no one would have imagined the scene taking place inside that peaceful-looking little house on the corner.

"Say them!" my father screamed. "Say them!"

The water was still running in the bathroom sink where I had started to get a drink, when my father grabbed me in his drunken rage.

"I can't, Daddy! I don't remember them!"

He raised his right hand high above his head and brought the palm down hard on my face. The blow sent me reeling into the large blue wastebasket my mother always kept near the sink. As the contents spilled out onto the floor, my father became even more incensed.

"Now look what you did! I'm going to beat you until you say them!"

There was no way to escape the viselike grip as he reached down and jerked me off the floor. I tried desperately to speak again, but the words would not come out.

Now he took off his leather belt and held it menacingly for me to see.

"You say your ABC's or I'll beat you black and blue!"

"Daddy, please, I can't!"

Too scared to resist, I stood numbly as my father raised the belt and brought it down across my back. Screaming with pain, I dropped in a heap on the floor as the blows continued to come, one after another. Finally, he picked me up by my shirt and carried me into my bedroom, throwing me onto the bed, ripping the buttons off my shirt as he did.

"You're stupid," he mumbled as he pulled the door shut and left my room. "My own son—stupid."

"Do you understand, Private Howland?" The colonel's

words brought me back to the present.

"Yes, Sir," I answered with just a touch of defiance in my voice.

The colonel shook his head and sighed resignedly, "You're dismissed. Go back to your company."

The discharge came four months later. The official reason was that I was "unadjustable to military life"—a civilized way to describe a loser. But I didn't care; I was glad to be out and away from the military discipline. My old feeling of restlessness had cropped up, and I wanted to be on the move again.

The restlessness that had plagued me throughout my adolescence stemmed from my boyhood. There had not only been innumerable beatings, but also we had moved constantly. Between my eighth and fourteenth birthdays, our family had lived in five states. I was constantly having to adjust to new schools, new neighborhoods, new friends because we were never in one place long enough to establish lasting relationships.

Dad was an alcoholic, but when he was sober he had a kind of charm that is hard to describe. He was a handsome man—short with black, wavy hair and dark eyes, fine features and a swarthy complexion. I guess he was what people used to call a "lady-killer." When he talked with people he sort of leaned toward them and gazed into their eyes as though he were taking in every word. Women loved it. So did men. Everybody did. He just had a way of making people feel as though they were very important and very interesting. And when he talked to them he always found an excuse for touching them. He'd lay his hand on a person's shoulder, or reach out and touch a woman's hand. He gave the impression that he was such a sympathetic guy, but this personality was the one he reserved for company and for those outside the family. At home he kicked off his shoes and drank and gave vent to all the bottled hate engendered by the day's frustrations and the annoyances which he had appeared to take with grace.

Dad was also an excellent tool and die-maker and was always able to find a good job. His ability, coupled with his winning personality, won him fast promotions, but after a few months on the job, his drinking problem would crop up, and we would be packing again.

Finally my mother and father were divorced, and both remarried. My two sisters, Norma and Shirley, and I remained with our mother, and in 1956 we settled for a time in Lincoln Park, Michigan, a suburb of Detroit. Those years of migratory existence, however, had created such a restlessness in me that I was not content to stay at home. I quit school and eight days after my seventeenth birthday I joined the army.

Now, after three years and eight months, I was out and free, wondering what new adventure life held. I was determined not to go home, no matter what. My stepfather had made it plain he did not want me coming home to live. "When kids get out on their own," he said, "they shouldn't come crawling back to Mama."

Within two weeks after my discharge, I had a letter from John Morton, saying that he had also been discharged and was living in Flint, Michigan. He was married and had a job as an inhalation therapist in a hospital. He invited me to come and stay with him and his wife, Clara, until I could find work. Having nothing better to do with my life, I accepted his invitation and headed for Flint. It was a decision that was to change my life.

*　　*　　*

John Morton and I had been together in France for nineteen months, and we had been best of friends from the first time we had met. John also came from a broken home, and had also lived in Fairborn, Ohio, when he was a youngster. We spent much of our spare time together, and the guys in the barracks often called us brothers.

John's younger brother, Tom, had recently been released from a federal institution for youthful offenders in Kentucky, and he was living just outside Flint. We got to be buddies because he had more free time than John had. He kept telling me how easy it was for him to get money quick. He had committed burglary and larceny on numerous occasions, and at times he and a companion went to a bar at night, waiting for the first unsuspecting drunk to come out of the tavern. Then one would grab him and hold him while the other took his wallet.

One night in late October Tom said, "Let's go to California." He and I had often talked of making such a trip.

"When?" I asked lazily.

"Right now. Tonight."

I had been working as an orderly in Flint General Hospital, but I was fired for striking a patient who had called me a dirty name. I guess the hospital thought the patient was in the wrong too because they discharged him because of the incident. Now I was "between jobs" and pretty bored. Just to take off and travel, footloose and fancy-free, sounded appealing.

"Have you got any cash?" I asked.

"No, but I know where we can get some fast, if you're willing," Tom was smiling, and I knew what he had in mind.

I drew a deep breath, then made my sudden decision.

"OK," I said. "Let's go!"

An hour later Tom and I were sitting in a parking lot, watching customers enter and leave a combination gas station and grocery store. Tom had worked there when he was in high school, and he estimated that the cash register would contain at least a thousand dollars in cash.

We sat in the car for about half an hour, mapping our strategy. The actual hold-up was to be my job alone, since Tom was afraid the owner or one of the employees might recognize him.

"Think you can do it?" Tom asked. He knew this was my first stick-up.

"I'll never know until I try!" I answered, getting out of the car with an air of bravado.

When I entered the store, I saw a middle-aged woman making change for a customer at the checkout counter. An old woman was sitting in a chair near the counter, but no other employee or customer was in sight.

Approaching the counter, I pulled a knife out of my pocket and showed it to the clerk at the register. "This is a stick-up," I announced. "Give me all the bills."

The clerk gasped and put her hand to her mouth to muffle a scream. Her hands were trembling as she opened the register and took out the bills. I grabbed the money and ran out the door. Tom pulled the car up by the door, and I jumped in. As we headed down the highway, I looked back but could see no one coming out of the store.

Tom gradually increased our speed until we were obviously going well over the speed limit.

"Slow down, man! Speeding is the best way to get caught!" I yelled.

"If you don't like my driving, you drive!" Tom said angrily, slamming on the brakes and pulling over to the side of the road.

"You sure pick a good time to get stubborn," I told him

as I got out and went around to the driver's side.

Keeping the car just under the speed limit, I began taking country roads at random, thinking the police would probably be watching the main highways. Tom counted the money.

"Not as much as I thought," he said. "One hundred and eight dollars."

"*A hundred and eight dollars!* I thought you said they kept a lot of money. That's a lousy amount to risk our necks for."

"It's too late to worry about that now," Tom responded glumly. "Let's just don't get caught."

We drove for the rest of the night. As we finally crossed the state line into Ohio, we breathed a sigh of relief.

Instead of going directly to California as we had planned, we headed east to Washington, D.C., and then south. Five days after leaving Michigan, we were in Columbia, South Carolina and were getting low on money. We found a gun-shop owner who was willing to sell us a .22-caliber pistol and a box of shells for our last twenty-five dollars. Then we embarked on a crime spree that carried us all the way across the United States.

Chapter
2

Dead End

Night was coming on as the bus pulled into the station just inside the California state line. The air was warm and clear, and the people waiting to board their buses were wearing short-sleeve shirts and summer dresses. I could hear the wail of a siren in the distance. Smiling at Tom I said, "Hear that? Maybe they're after us."

"Give us a break, Man. We just got here," Tom replied, pulling a cigarette out of his shirt pocket. He lit up, and we walked through the station and out the front door onto Main Street.

We stopped at a street corner and looked around. In the block ahead we could see a long line forming in front of a movie theater. Most of the stores were still open, their bright lights and open doors inviting everyone to come in and examine their wares.

"We need a car first of all," Tom said, turning to me. "Got any great ideas of where to start?" Our car had developed mechanical trouble the night before, and we had left it parked along the road somewhere in Arizona.

"You're the expert," I said. "You tell me." Tom took a deep drag on his cigarette before he answered. He glanced around at the people hurrying past us—people who evidently had families to go home to or important dates to keep. We had neither. We were just a couple of drifters who had embarked on a career of crime four weeks ago, and had been on the run ever since.

Before abandoning our car we had broken into a church. Tom had handed me a lug wrench.

"Break the window in the door, then put your hand in and see if you can reach the doorknob," he said.

I closed my eyes and smashed the window. It seemed to make a tremendous amount of noise, and my heart was pounding for fear someone would catch us.

My hands were trembling and wet with sweat when I turned the knob, and we walked in. As we moved through the dark building I rammed my hip against a doorknob on another door. Turning our flashlight on the door I saw a sign that read "Pastor's Study." With my full weight I pushed against the door and heard the wood tear from the hinges.

We ransacked the office, looking for cash. There was none. Looking back now, I can remember the uncomfortable feeling that crept over me when Tom suggested we take the typewriter and try to sell it. "No," I had said. "We need money, not typewriters."

What had gotten into me? Why that strange, creepy feeling? "Aw, forget it!" I told myself. "That was last night. This is another day, and we *still* need money and a car."

Tom's voice brought me out of my reverie. "Let's start walking down one of these side streets. We'll find something."

Soon we were in a pleasant residential area with neat, well-cared-for lawns and shrubs. A tricycle sat on the sidewalk across the street, left by its owner to face the perils of the night. Most of the houses had lights on and the windows open. Television programs could be heard blaring from several of the homes.

A few cars were parked along the street. As we approached each one, I kept watch while Tom looked to see if the keys had been left in the ignition. In our brief career as partners in crime, we had already committed armed robbery and burglary, as well as just plain theft. Stealing a car seemed to be a pretty simple operation.

At the end of the block Tom checked the last car, then joined me beside a large hedge.

"None of them got keys in them. Let's check the alley," Tom said.

We circled the half-block and turned into a narrow alley, where several cars were parked. "The perfect place to look," I thought.

The third car we checked had the keys in it. Motioning for me to be quiet, Tom pointed toward the house. Excitement coursed through my whole being. On a screened back porch, the family was sitting around a table, evidently engaged in some game. Tom slipped behind the wheel, and I quietly opened the door on the other side and got in.

"Here goes nothing," Tom whispered. He turned the key, and the car started immediately. There was only one problem: it didn't have a muffler, and the noise was practically deafening.

As Tom shut the engine off, I saw the man on the screened porch jump up from the table and move for the door.

"Let's get out of here!" I muttered. We both scrambled out of the car and took off down the alley. After running until we were out of breath, we stopped and looked back. No one was following.

"Man, that was close!" Tom panted.

"Too close—but what do we do now? We've got to do something or we'll never get out of here," I said. "Let's see how much money we have."

Standing under a streetlight, we counted our pooled resources. Together we had seven pennies, a dime and a five-cent piece.

"Well, at least we've got this, Larry," Tom said as he patted the left pocket of his jacket. He was referring to the pistol—practically our only possession.

"Yeah, but I'd trade it for a good ride right now. Come on! Let's look for another car."

After walking about six blocks we finally came upon an old model Chevrolet parked in front of a modern apartment house. Across the street was a vacant lot. Except for a gentle wind blowing the foot-high weeds on the lot, there seemed to be no activity. "Come on, Larry," Tom said. "It doesn't have the key in it, but the ignition is on. Hop in; I'll drive."

"I sure hope this one has a good muffler," I told him as I got in on the passenger's side.

Tom started the car, and the engine purred to life. As we eased away from the curb, I reached over and switched on the radio. The news was on, and I started turning the dial to find some rock music. Tom's voice broke in over the sound of the static: "Tonight's just not our night."

"What's the matter?"

"No brakes!"

"What! Come on, Man, knock it off!"

"Naw, look for yourself."

I looked down and saw that Tom had the brake pedal all the way to the floor. I braced myself as we ran through a red light, and finally coasted safely to a stop.

"Whew! I whistled. "There's got to be something worth stealing around here."

"Maybe we'd better walk," Tom suggested.

"Sure, smart guy—all the way across the state!"

I thought about those words. Actually we didn't even know *where* we were going. We were just *going*. We were thinking about going to the state of Washington, but we really had no purpose or goal. We just stole enough to get us to the next place—then stole again.

Finding another residential street, we started once more on the routine of checking each car. Finally I came across a newer-model Falcon with the keys left in it. I called Tom, and this time I took the wheel.

"Take it easy," Tom said softly. "The people are sitting right there in the living room."

"That's all right," I laughed. "In a minute they won't have anything to chase us with."

"You're crazy, Man!"

"Yeah, I think we both are."

The car started quietly, and the people inside didn't even notice as we pulled away. "See! You just have to know how to do it," I bragged.

We headed southwest, not really knowing where we were going, but just taking whatever road appealed to us. After we had driven for about an hour, I noticed that the gas gauge was heading toward empty. I wondered what we should do. Tom was slumped down in the seat, smoking the last of our cigarettes and chewing on a stick of gum he had found in the glove compartment.

"Say, Pal, I hate to bring you back to reality, but we're about out of gas."

"You want to rob some place?" Tom inquired, blowing smoke in my direction.

"With *this* thing?" I asked unbelievingly. "Man, you

couldn't outrun a wheelbarrow with this! We'd get caught for sure. I don't know what we should do just yet."

"Maybe we can find another car," Tom suggested.

"Yeah, I guess that's the only solution."

We were coming into a small resort town. It was getting late now, and no one seemed to be up. Only a few customers remained in the local bar, and the skating rink was empty and dark. Just after we passed the rink, we spotted a Chevrolet camper parked off the road, about thirty feet from a cluster of tourist cabins. I eased up beside it, and Tom got out and looked in the cab. "The ignition's on," he told me. "I'll back it out."

"You better check and see if anyone's in the back," I cautioned. Tom walked to the back of the camper and peeked in the window. "It's too dark to tell, Larry, but there wouldn't be anyone in there. It probably belongs to someone in one of those cabins." There were several cabins half hidden in a grove of tall trees.

Tom backed the truck out while I parked the Falcon on the side of the road. Then I climbed into the cab with Tom, and once again we were on our way. Finding the glove compartment unlocked, I opened it and began examining the contents.

"Hey, Tom, look what I found!" I yelled.

"What is it, Man?"

"A checkbook. Not only that, but there must be thirty checks here."

"Hey!" Tom said happily. "That solves all our problems."

"Yeah, it shouldn't be hard to pass these off. With this many checks, we can make them out for small amounts. It ought to be easy to cash a check for twenty or thirty dollars."

I wasn't worried about what we would use for identification, or the fact that they were out-of-state checks. I knew that we could cash them somehow, even if we had to be a little persuasive.

"I'll let you do the cashing," Tom grinned.

"Thanks, Pal! I appreciate that."

I looked over at the speedometer and saw that we were going about sixty-five. The speed limit was only fifty. "Hey!" I told him. "Slow this thing down, or else pull over and let me drive. You're going to wreck us, or get us stopped for speeding!"

"You worry too much," Tom replied, but he slowed down.

Now that we had the truck and the checkbook we began to make big plans. What more could a guy ask for? We had it made!

Then without warning, the road came to a dead end. There was nothing to do but turn around and go back the way we had come. I knew we had been traveling south. "Must be the Mexican border," I told Tom. "But it seems like there would be. . . ."

I stopped, suddenly interrupted by a tapping noise on the window behind us. Cold sweat engulfed my body, as Tom turned to me with a look of panic on his face. "What was that?"

"I don't know!" Turning, I looked into the window of the camper just as a light came on inside it. What I saw made my blood run cold. "There's a guy back there!" I yelled. "And he's got a gun!"

Tom gasped. "Can you jump?" he asked.

"Yeah. Let's get out of here!" Frantically, I searched for the door handle, but before I could find it, the world exploded in my ear. *Tom had been shot!* His body slumped over the steering wheel like a sack of potatoes. As the truck stalled, I yanked my door open and jumped out.

The man in the back was on the ground as fast as I was. I stopped and faced him, putting my hands up. I couldn't see him very well, but I could see the barrel of the gun pointed toward me. "What are you up to?" he hissed at me.

I couldn't answer. I just stood there, frozen. Then I saw him bring the gun up to his shoulder, and I knew he was going to shoot me too. I started to turn and run even though I knew there was no escape, no place to go. I never made that turn. There was another explosion, and I felt as if I had been hit in both legs with a huge club—only for some reason it didn't hurt. The force seemed to lift me off my feet, and the next moment I was lying on my back in a warm, sticky pool of my own blood.

I could hear the man's steps as he walked toward me. I saw him point the gun at my head. "Who are you?" he growled.

I didn't answer. I don't think I could have. I just covered my face and head with both arms as best I could and held my breath, knowing that any second he might pull the trigger again.

Then, unexpectedly, I heard him walking away from me, back toward the camper.

I tried to get up, but I couldn't. The slightest movement of my legs brought intense pain. I wondered if Tom was still alive.

"Tom!" I yelled. "Tom! Tom!" There was only silence.

Then I did something I hadn't done for a long, long time. I prayed. "Lord, help me!" I pleaded. "Lord, if You will only help me now, I'll be Yours forever!"

My thoughts went back to my childhood. Our family was not what you would call a Christian family, but I had felt God's hand upon me. I remembered that once when I was just a little kid I had felt that God wanted me to be a preacher. But I had never responded to that call, never yielded my life to God. Even so, as I lay there in the dirt, praying out of sheer desperation, I had a strange assurance that God was listening to me.

I continued alternately praying and calling Tom's name until the sheriff came with the ambulance, and two men began to put me onto a stretcher.

"Tom," I muttered. "My buddy Tom. Take care of him first."

Someone walked around the front of the truck and quickly returned.

"Is Tom OK?" I asked.

"He's dead," the man said. "Sorry, kid."

Chapter

3

Murder?

I tried to force my eyes open. Everything was hazy, but even before I could see clearly, I knew where I was. The antiseptic smell of a hospital was unmistakable. My hand went immediately to my legs. They were still there, but the right one was encased in a large cast. Turning my head, I saw someone sitting in a chair beside the bed. I couldn't quite make out who it was, and the chair seemed to be moving back and forth. I wished it would stand still.

"How are you feeling?" The voice was as unmistakable—and almost as unwelcome—as the hospital odor. It was that of my father, who lived just outside of Los Angeles. I tried to answer "OK," but I wasn't sure that my lips succeeded in forming the word.

My father's voice unleashed a flood of memories. It seemed that I was no longer twenty-one years old and lying in a hospital bed, but six years old and sitting up in my bed at home, screaming "Mommy! Mommy!" I had been awakened by a horn blaring outside and a man's voice yelling hysterically, "I'll kill you! I swear I'll kill you! I'll teach you to mess with my wife!" My sister Norma came running into the room and grabbed me.

"There's a man outside with a gun, and he's trying to shoot Daddy!" she sobbed.

I started screaming louder as Norma and I clutched each other in panic, listening for the shot that never came. Then we heard a siren and knew that the police were on the way. I buried my head in my sister's shoulder—afraid to learn what had happened. Finally my mother came in and picked me up. "It's OK," she said, sobbing. "The police took them to jail. Oh, I don't know *why* your father runs around like that!" She was trembling, and she held me very tight.

Suddenly I was back in the hospital room, with my father sitting in a chair looking at me. I still didn't know if I had answered him, so I tried again to say, "OK." Once more the room faded away and I was back at home, crying and screaming, "No, Daddy, no! I promise not to do it anymore!" Then I seemed to hear him yelling at me, "Get your clothes on! I'm taking you to the doctor and having you operated on. You've wet the bed for the last time in this house!"

"No, no!" I screamed and ran for my mother. She sheltered me in her arms.

"Jimmy," she said, "you shouldn't scare him like this! It's not healthy to do that."

"He's going to learn not to wet the bed if I have to beat him . . . ."

The hospital room came briefly into focus again, and then there was darkness. I thought I was being jerked out of bed. Now we were in the car, and my mother was driving too fast. "Where are we going?" I whimpered. "What's the matter?"

My mother rushed me into a large room that smelled like medicine. She was crying as the doctor put me on the examining table. "I woke up," I heard her sob, "and he was making a grinding noise with his teeth and he was foaming at the mouth. What's wrong with him, Doctor? What's *wrong?*" She was almost hysterical. That scene faded, and now I was eavesdropping on an earnest conversation between my parents. "Jimmy, those tests showed nothing wrong with Larry. The doctor says it was just nerves . . . . You're going to have to quit your drinking, Jimmy. I'm telling you, we can't take it any longer. That boy is going to end up in a mental institution!"

. . . Slowly the hospital room came back into focus—and this time my dad's chair didn't seem to be moving. He asked again, "How do you feel?"

"OK," I said.

"I came right away when I found out." He shifted nervously in his chair and began to carry on an awkward, one-sided conversation: How had I gotten myself into this mess? What would my mother think? Look at my future now! I was beginning to drift back into unconsciousness when he suddenly said something that jolted me awake:

"By the way—I don't understand. Who did you murder?"

I stiffened on the bed. "Wh-what do you mean, who did I murder?"

"Well," he said, "the sheriff told me they have you charged with auto theft, kidnapping, and second-degree murder. I don't know what the murder charge is based on. The sheriff said he'd know more about the charges later this afternoon."

His voice went on, but I quit listening. My mind raced back to the events of the night before. Or was it last week? What had happened? We didn't kill anyone. My dad broke in on my thoughts as he stood up to leave.

"I have to go, Larry, but I'll be back."

34

"Yeah, sure," I said weakly.

"And listen, Larry," he went on, "you remember one thing."

"What's that?" I asked politely. Man, I wished he would go away!

"You keep your mouth shut, and don't tell them anything. I'll see if I can get you a lawyer."

I didn't answer, but I tried to manage a nod. After he left, I did some thinking about his final words of advice. I knew I wasn't a Christian, but I had prayed and asked God to get me out of this mess. I didn't think He'd want me to hold back information. Tom was dead, so I was the only one who might be hurt by any information I gave. And I was tired of running—so tired. I decided that I would try to be completely honest with the police.

My religious background was a dead zero. The only person in my family who ever went to church was my Aunt Thelma. She went every Sunday to a Wesleyan church. I stayed with her one time while my folks were on vacation, and she took me to church along with her son and her two daughters. Sometimes I would look back on that visit, and I would remember that Sunday, and I would think it must be nice to be a preacher. It was a Walter Mitty daydream. I would imagine myself in the pulpit with a big Bible open in front of me, and I would be telling people to "get right with God, Brethren!"

Actually, I did have a little exposure to religion when I was in my teens. My stepfather was a Lutheran and he would go to church once in awhile. And just before the end of my junior year in high school he enrolled me in the Detroit Lutheran High West. I went there until I quit, part-way through my senior year. I was probably the only kid in the school who didn't know the Lord's Prayer and had never read the Bible. I felt like a fool.

35

I was thinking about the months at Lutheran High when the guard stepped into my room. He was a small man with black hair and a little scar over his upper lip. He asked, "How're you doing?"

"All right, I guess. Say, is there any way I could see a minister?"

He took off his cap and scratched his head with it. "Gee, I don't know. Never had anyone ask before. But I'll sure check for you."

"Thanks a lot," I said sleepily.

"Mr. Howland . . . Mr. Howland . . . ." It seemed as if only five minutes had passed. I could hear a voice, but I couldn't seem to get my eyes open. When I finally did, I saw a small, bald man standing there smiling down at me.

"I'm Mr. Harris," he said. "I was told you wanted to see a minister."

Sweat broke out on my forehead. Now that the minister was here, I wished he would go away. I didn't know what to say to him.

"I guess I'm in a little trouble," I finally began.

"Tell me what happened, Son."

Once the ice was broken, I found myself talking to him freely. "You probably won't believe this," I said, after awhile, "but when I was a kid I used to want to be a minister. I'm not even a Christian, but somehow I just had that feeling."

"It's not too late, Larry," he said gently. "God can still use you. Why don't we have a word of prayer together?"

I nodded my agreement, and the minister began to pray. His prayer made God seem so near—much nearer than when I had prayed lying in the road.

"O Heavenly Father," Mr. Harris began, "please reach down and touch Your servant this day. May Your forgiveness be upon him. Guide and direct his path and have

Your sovereign way in his life. We pray in Thy Son's holy name. Amen."

I could almost feel God touching me with a strong and gentle hand.

Mr. Harris stood up and took my hand. "If I can help you in any way, you just call."

After he left I fell into a peaceful sleep.

On Wednesday, five days after I had been admitted to the hospital, a detective came to question me. He brought along a secretary who wrote down all the details as I related them. I confessed to the robberies, the burglaries, and even to breaking into the church and ransacking the pastor's study looking for money. To my surprise, I found it very painful to confess to crimes that I had formerly boasted about. For the first time in many years, I was aware of having a conscience.

When the detective handed me the statement to sign, he promised, "You won't regret being honest with us."

"I don't know," I sighed. "How can I beat a murder rap? And why am I charged with murder anyhow? I haven't killed anybody!"

"In the state of California, Mr. Howland, if anyone is killed in the commission of a felony, the other felons are held responsible. In other words, you're responsible for Tom's death."

My heart seemed to stop.

I tried to prop myself up on my elbow. "You're putting me on!" I said angrily. "Tom was my buddy! Man, I didn't want anything to happen to Tom! How can you pin his death on me?"

"I'm sorry, Mr. Howland, but that's the law."

I lay back down. All of a sudden I forgot my desire to do right. It was one thing to be honest, but another to take a bum rap.

As the detective gathered up his papers, I said sarcastically, "Nice state!"

"We think so," he replied. "And we want to keep it that way."

He walked out of the room, then turned and came back. "By the way," he said, "they will be transferring you back to the county in which you committed the crimes as soon as you are able to travel."

"Did the doctor say when that would be?" I asked.

I would have preferred staying where I was, so that I could call on Mr. Harris when I needed help, but I couldn't stop the healing process.

On Saturday I was transferred to a smaller hospital 150 miles away. When I arrived there by ambulance in the sheriff's custody, I was told that I would have to be put in the psychiatric ward, since the hospital had no facilities for prisoners.

I spent the next several weeks in isolation, with nothing to read and nothing to do but think. The only time I saw the hall outside my door was when the doctor came to examine me. The food was passed in to me through a small window in the door. As I lay there alone, I wondered time and again just how much trouble I had gotten myself into.

One day a heavy-set man with a very serious look on his face was shown into my room. Bringing a chair in with him he sat down beside my bed.

"My name is Mr. Ingram," he told me, "and I have been appointed to represent you at your trial."

"Did my dad send you?" I asked.

"No, I have been appointed by the court."

"Well, I'm glad to have someone on my side," I said, closing my eyes. I think I had known all along that my dad's promise was just an attempt to sound like a concerned father.

"Yes. Well now, I've talked to the district attorney, and I believe we have worked out a reasonable solution."

"What's that supposed to mean?"

"The district attorney has been very generous, Mr. Howland. Your crimes are capital offenses and are punishable by a maximum penalty of death."

"*What?*" I sputtered. "What do you mean—death?"

"Mr. Howland, you have committed some serious crimes. The D.A. has agreed to drop the murder and kidnapping charges if you will plead guilty to the charge of auto theft."

I was getting mad, and it showed. "You mean he'll do all those nice things for me?" My sarcasm failed to hide the fear his words had aroused.

"Yes, and I would advise you to accept the proposition," Mr. Ingram told me very seriously. "If you don't, I'm sure you will regret it."

"Well," I said doubtfully, "I'm guilty, there's no doubt about it. But I don't have any past record. It looks like they would take that into consideration."

"They have," he replied. "That's the only reason the D.A. has agreed to drop the murder and kidnapping charges."

"What can I get out of the auto-theft charge?" I asked.

"It's an automatic sentence—six months to five years. And then, of course, at the end of that term you will have to face charges in two other states that have issued warrants for your arrest." He snapped shut his brief case.

After Mr. Ingram left, I lay there and thought about what he had said. The death sentence was unthinkable; I couldn't even imagine it. But I could well imagine being locked in a cell for long, long years. Even as I contemplated it, I began to yearn for open fields and sunshine and wide, wide skies. How could I live without them—I, who had always had a wanderlust? How could I bear to be imprisoned like a lion in a cage? How could I endure the crowding, the discipline, the dull routine? Already my heart was breaking, and there was no one to talk with, no one who cared about me.

Then I recalled how I had almost felt God's hand on the top of my head the day Mr. Harris prayed for me. As I recalled the sweetness of the moment God again seemed very near, and I turned to Him.

"God," I said, choking on my fear and my sorrow. That was all I said. There were no words for what I was feeling. "God!" I cried. "God! God!" It was a cry from the very depths of my soul.

A peace swept over me—cool and gentle as a silken scarf, it wrapped itself around me.

Slowly I began to realize that God had indeed moved in my behalf, and I wished I could get down on my knees to thank Him. I knew that the district attorney's decision to drop those charges against me was dictated by Someone with power far greater than his.

All of the trial procedures were taken care of in the hospital. They rolled my bed into a room where a temporary court had been set up. After several preliminaries, the judge looked at me and asked, "Mr. Howland, how do you plead?"

My mouth was dry. "Guilty, Your Honor."

The sentence imposed by the judge was just what Mr. Ingram had told me it would be: six months to five years in prison. Six weeks after my dead-end ride, I was on my way to the prison reception center at Chino, California.

Chapter

4

San Quentin

After spending six weeks in the prison hospital at Chino, I was released from the reception center along with about twenty other prisoners. We were shackled with chains and loaded onto a prison bus to be transported to San Quentin Prison at Tamal, California.

Rough as it was, the 350-mile trip was all too short. I gazed out the window, drinking in everything I could see, trying to stamp it on my memory for future reference. I wanted a bank of mental pictures to draw on, to keep me sane until I was free again. Every sight was precious; I didn't want to miss a thing: the girls on street corners, waiting for the light to change; the red and white signs for "this week's specials" plastered on the windows of a supermarket; lines of telephone poles with wires looped between them in long, gentle curves; a hawk gliding over a cow pasture; a young mother pushing a blue stroller with a little kid in it. I hoarded every scene.

When our bus turned off the highway onto the road leading to the prison gate, my heart sank. I could see the massive pink walls, the towers, the locked gates. I tried to shut off the camera in my mind; it was one picture I did not want to carry with me.

Armed guards observed our bus as it pulled up to the gate. The gate opened, and we drove inside. Then the gate closed behind us.

The reception area was a large room built into the prison wall itself. As we stood there, dejected and thirsty, a short, stocky guard who was chewing on an unlighted cigar mumbled our names in alphabetical order.

"Howland."

"Here."

Another guard then removed the chains from my hands and feet. I moved my wrists and my ankles to get the kinks out of them.

Another guard then took charge.

"Ok, strip all your clothes off. You can't take nothin' with you. Anything you don't want to mail home will be thrown away."

A clean-cut looking prisoner standing next to me called himself "Doc." Now he spoke up to the guard.

"Wait a minute! What about our smokes?"

"You heard me," the guard replied gruffly. "You can't take nothin' with you."

"Just my luck," Doc muttered to me. "I bought a carton of cigarettes yesterday so I would have some when we got here."

I grinned at him weakly. I was so frightened that I didn't trust myself to speak. All of the first-timers felt the same way.

In the reception center at Chino, we had heard how rough San Quentin is. We had heard about the murders and the homosexuals. The average age of the prisoners in San Quentin, we were told, is thirty-one years. It was said that few of the younger and weaker inmates get by very long without being victimized in some way. Many of them are "turned out"—that means they are physically forced into becoming the passive partner in a homosexual act.

I had just reached my twenty-first birthday. In California most of the younger convicts are sent to Soledad Prison, but because I was wanted in two other states I was considered a security risk and consequently was assigned to serve my time in San Quentin.

We were each given a shirt, a pair of pants, and a pair of shoes, and we were told to put them on.

"Ok," the guard said, "follow me and we'll issue you some underwear and bedding."

We followed him through the gate and into the main prison area. As the old-timers saw us coming, they began to shout and whistle.

"Hey, look at the fish!" one yelled.

"*Welcome to the capitol of hell!*" another inmate called out.

Because of my limp, I was at the back of the group. Feeling vulnerable and alone, I hurried to catch up.

In the supply room, we received our convicts' uniforms and other wearing apparel, along with sheets, blankets, and a pillowcase. Then we were given our cell numbers and taken to our cells in the South Block. This is the maximum security part of the prison, where all new inmates are sent until they are processed. I.D. cards have to be issued, jobs found for each convict who can work, and each inmate classified according to the crime he has committed, the amount of time he is to serve, and other considerations.

As I followed the other men down the catwalk, I looked for my cell. A short fellow a few years older than I, was standing in front of 4639. As I waited for the door to be unlocked, he turned to me.

"You lock here?" he asked.

"Yeah, I guess so."

"Then I guess we're gonna be cell partners. My name's Eddie Grayson." We shook hands.

It was comforting to see a smiling face, and I liked Eddie right away. He was, I think, about three years older than I. He never talked about his family, but he did tell me that he was single. I don't even know what his occupation had been. Maybe he never had an occupation. He had spent most of his life in prison. He had served time in Tennessee, and now he was in San Quentin for robbery. His term was five years to life. Besides that, he was wanted in another state for an assault charge stemming from a shootout. But he was a nice guy. He wasn't mean or sullen the way some of the inmates were. He was always wise-cracking and playing harmless little jokes. I really liked him.

The next morning we were taken to breakfast and then told that we were free to walk around the prison yard until a job was assigned to us. The "upper yard," in the middle of the four cell blocks, is about the size of a football field and is covered by a large sheet-metal roof where the inmates can seek shelter when it rains. The "lower yard" is open and much larger with a baseball diamond in it. While I was "inspecting" the upper yard, some sea gulls flew down and walked fearlessly among the prisoners, eating the bread which many of the convicts had brought from the mess hall. My heart leaped at the sight of the birds, and I planned to save some bread for them so I could feed them too.

I was standing alone at the edge of the upper yard, wishing I could be feeding the gulls right then, when a cross-eyed fellow with peculiar mannerisms walked up to me. He waved at me, and his wrist snapped daintily, the

44

way a girl's wrist does when she waves.

"Hi, honey, what's your name?" he said in a throaty voice.

"Larry," I said. I was afraid not to answer.

"Where ya from?"

"Detroit," I said uncomfortably. I had wished for somebody to talk with, but I hadn't bargained for this.

"Oh, really? Me and my husband used to live there."

"Yeah, Ok," I mumbled, edging away from him. As I glanced over my shoulder to make certain he wasn't following me, I saw several inmates bent over with laughter, enjoying the initiation I had just received.

I found Eddie and told him what had happened. He laughed at me too.

"What's so funny?" I said.

"Aw, that's Penny Mae, Larry. She's a queen. Don't play so dumb."

The fact is that I was not playing dumb at all. I really didn't know much about homos. I had heard some dirty jokes about them and some scary stories, but I had never been around any before.

As time went by, I found out that Penny Mae was only one of many so-called queens in the prison. They were among the most pitiful inmates I met. Many of them were homosexuals by choice, but others had been "turned out" by older and stronger inmates. It was not unusual for a young fellow to be given a choice: submit to a homosexual act or be stabbed.

The cells are designed for two men, and homosexual partners often request to live together. Out of a desire to preserve harmony, the officials usually honor such requests. Only if immoral conduct is actually observed by a guard are the men punished. The perversion and depravity I witnessed during those first weeks in San Quentin

45

made me feel that I had indeed arrived at the capitol of hell.

Prison life quickly developed into a routine. From Monday through Friday we were let out of our cells to work seven hours a day on the job assigned to us. I had a job doing office work. During the lunch hour we were free to roam the yard and engage in sports activities such as basketball or handball, or to go to the gymnasium and use the equipment there. When it was warm, many inmates simply lay out in the sun in the lower yard.

After supper each evening, we were locked in our cells at 6 P. M. and remained there until breakfast time. On Saturdays and Sundays we were released from our cells and were free to engage in any activities available within the prison. Certain parts of the prison are restricted, however, and we could go into these areas only with a pass.

Among the restricted areas are the two blocks where the honor prisoners live—North Block and West Block. Life for the inmates of these cell blocks is a little easier. On the bottom floor of the five tiers, television areas and a barber shop are available for their use. They are also permitted to visit in each other's cells, although it is against the rules for a visitor to go past the foot of the bunk.

Recognizing the advantages of being an honor prisoner, I set out to earn this status through good behavior. After four months, I was moved to North Block. Although Eddie also requested to move to North Block, he was refused without explanation.

I had learned early that it paid to have friends. Guys who were "loners" got into trouble fast. Eddie and I had become good friends with Doc, who claimed to be a medical doctor from Los Angeles; with a young fellow from Wisconsin named Wendy; and with another convict named Kincaid, who was in for passing bad checks. The five of us looked after each other.

One hot afternoon we had a chance to prove our loyalty. As we were getting lined up for supper, Wendy came walking up to Kincaid and me. He was breathing heavily and looking nervously over his shoulder.

"I'm in trouble," he muttered under his breath.

"What's the matter?" I could see he was really afraid.

"Some guy told me he and his buddies would get me if I didn't turn over my stuff from the canteen on Saturday."

The prison currency, issued once a month, is given in the form of "ducats." Each inmate is paid a nominal amount for the work he does on the job assigned him in prison. The top pay when I was in San Quentin was twenty-six cents an hour—barely enough to purchase a few luxuries at the canteen each month. Each inmate's ducats have his name and number imprinted on them, and we had to show our I.D. cards (which had our pictures on them) to make a purchase at the canteen.

Since this system makes it almost impossible to spend someone else's ducats, the inmate-extortioners, known as "gunsels," make their victim buy his goods and then they take them from him. They even prey on physically handicapped prisoners who are not able to resist.

"Quit worrying," I told Wendy. "We'll make sure they don't bother you."

"What you gonna do, Man?"

I could see they had really frightened Wendy. He was still shaking.

"I said don't worry. We're with you all the way."

"OK, OK," he said. But I knew he was still scared, and I knew also that he had good reason to be. Guys had been killed for refusing to turn over their goods. Wendy stuck with us so closely the rest of the week that we began to think we had a shadow.

Saturday came quickly—too quickly, as far as Wendy was concerned. He grew more jittery as the day approached. On Friday he was given another warning: Pay up or else.

When the canteen opened, Doc, Kincaid, and I went with Wendy and waited for him as he came out with a large bag of items. As he was approaching us, a tall black suddenly stepped in front of him. Several others appeared on either side of him and behind him.

We got to Wendy just as the guy standing in front of him said, "OK, hand it over."

"Beat it, Punk!" Kincaid said. Reaching in front of the black, he grabbed Wendy's bag.

The black guy threw a punch at Wendy, but missed. Wendy started to swing back, and it looked as if we were in for a fight that could develop into a big racial flare-up. Unexpectedly the tall guy said, "All right, Man, all right! Don't get so uptight about it. I was just teasing."

"Beat it, Punk!" Doc told him again.

The blacks glared at us and then walked away. We breathed a sigh of relief.

"Man, that was close!" Doc said.

"Yeah," I agreed, and headed for the lower yard to sit peacefully on the bleachers and be thankful for another day of life.

The racial tension seemed to grow worse. Once in awhile it would flare up, and an inmate would be stabbed with a "shiv," a homemade knife made in the prison from metal taken out of the machine shop or out of a toilet. Sometimes they were made from pieces of formica taken from the furniture factory. Occasionally an inmate was beaten to death with a pipe or some other instrument. We lived in constant fear for our lives. Racial fights were apt to erupt at any moment, and could quickly develop into major riots. In 1967, two years after I left San Quentin, fourteen inmates were injured in a race riot which involved almost 3,000 prisoners.

Not all of the murders in San Quentin were racially motivated, however. Prisoners were killed because they were unable to pay off gambling debts, or for trying to steal someone's queen. Murders became so frequent that officials began photographing the corpses at the murder scene and posted the pictures with a large sign that read, "**DID YOU MAKE THE SHIV THAT DID THIS?**" Inmates would gather around the pictures for long periods of time, seemingly fascinated by them. Posting such pictures was a morbid procedure that never produced any results—a prisoner would be crazy to admit that he had supplied a murderer with his weapon.

Without some means of escaping temporarily from the harsh realities of existence at San Quentin, many of the inmates would probably go berserk. Work offered some relief from the tensions of prison life. I was given a job as billing clerk in the furniture factory, where I prepared the invoices and mailed them out to purchasers across the state.

Some prisoners take advantage of the educational opportunities available to them. Classes are offered on the remedial, elementary, and high-school level. The state will also finance a correspondence course for an honor inmate who wants to earn college credits.

For some prisoners, involvement in religious activities serves as a form of escape, if nothing more. Various denominational groups come into the prison during the evening hours, and prisoners who are not in close or maximum security can get permission to attend one of these functions each week.

The free movie shown once a week in the mess hall gives many of the prisoners an opportunity to take a two-hour "trip" away from life at San Quentin. Inmates with vivid imaginations are able to take such a trip more often for each bunk is equipped with a headset tuned in to a radio station that offers a variety of music, ranging from classical to country and Western. I spent many evenings just lying on my bunk, listening to the music and reliving the happier memories of my childhood.

My thoughts often went back to Fairborn, Ohio, where we had lived until I was eight years old. I remembered the many deep snows of winter and the warm evenings of summer, when we would play outside until dark. I recalled the excitement with which I looked forward to the visits of a family friend who owned an old car with a rumble seat. Sometimes I could almost feel the wind blowing on my face and hear the voices of my sisters, Shirley and Norma, as we laughed and shouted to each other over the assorted noises made by the rattletrap car. Now both of my sisters had families and were happy and content. All I could do from San Quentin was be happy for them and, at the same time, be somewhat envious.

Another memory that kept recurring was that of running down the sidewalk into the outstretched arms of Grandma and Grandpa Howland. My father had been born out of wedlock and was cruelly neglected by the people who were caring for him. Grandpa was doing some carpentry work at their house and overheard them discussing ways of getting rid of the unwanted infant. Grandpa said, "If you don't want that baby, I'll take him!" So he and Grandma adopted my father, and loved him and cared for him as though he were their own natural child. They showered the same sweet affection on me, and supplied me with the happy memories of my childhood.

They were dead now, and I still missed them, but I was glad they had not lived to see me become a convicted criminal.

Thoughts of my mother always brought me back to the present with a jolt. I had put off writing to her because I hated for her to receive a letter from me with San Quentin as a return address. Even though a brief note from Norma had told me that she and my mother had been informed of my arrest and hospitalization, I kept hoping that Mom didn't know where I was imprisoned. Only after several weeks had gone by did I finally get the courage to write Mom—thankful that I didn't have to see the mixture of relief and hurt in her eyes when she received my letter.

Chapter
5

The Chaplain and The Witnesses

During my first three months in San Quentin, I kept thinking about the prayer I had prayed the night I was shot—but I just didn't know what I should do about it. Although I got a Bible from the prison library and read it often, I didn't seem to find the guidance I was seeking. Remembering how I had been helped by the minister who visited me in the hospital, I finally made an appointment to see one of the two Protestant chaplains in the prison.

The chaplain's waiting room was neatly furnished and smelled of fresh paint. An inmate-clerk looked up from his typing and told me to have a seat. After I had waited a few minutes, the chaplain—a middle-aged man in a gray business suit—came out to greet me.

"Come on into my office," he said cordially, shaking my hand.

As we started back into his private office, he turned and said to his clerk, "By the way, I went over to the hospital to see John Nix, and he was sure _____ed up."

I could hardly believe my ears. He had used the vilest

four-letter word I knew. Surely a man of God would not stoop so low! Not noticing my reaction, he ushered me into his office and offered me a seat.

"Forget it, Chaplain," I told him. "I've changed my mind."

I turned and walked out—disheartened, disillusioned and discouraged.

A few weeks later, I was summoned before the parole board and informed that I could be paroled within two months. The elation I felt when I heard that news was short-lived. The chairman of the parole board went on to say, "Mr. Howland, you will be released to the custody of either Georgia or Michigan, the two states that have warrants for you. We're not sure yet which one will have first claim."

I sat there stunned. "I won't sign any waivers," I said finally.

"Then, Mr. Howland," the chairman replied, "we will keep you here until you are ready to sign, or until you've served your full five-year sentence. It's up to you."

I went back to my cell as dejected as I had ever been. "O God!" I cried out in despair. "Where are You?" The cell walls gave no answer.

For the next few days, I lived a hopeless existence. At times my mind turned to thoughts of suicide—but I seemed to lack even the initiative to plan and carry out this means of escaping from the mess I had gotten myself into. It looked as if I might have to spend an endless lifetime in prison.

One day as I sat dejectedly in my chair at work, my boss, Mr. Goldstein, came to my desk, carrying a handful of invoices.

"We need these in a hurry," he said. The noise from a saw in the furniture factory below us almost drowned out his words.

I was glad to have the work. It made time go faster and helped me to get my mind off the future. I was about half through with the invoices when someone spoke to me: "Come on, Larry—coffee time."

I looked up and saw Doc standing in front of my desk. He worked in the office with me, and was responsible for the payroll of inmates in the industrial section of the prison.

"OK, Man, let's go," I replied. We walked into the back room, where hot coffee was always waiting.

Doc's story was an interesting one. He and his wife were on the brink of divorce. She had developed such a hatred for him that she wanted to hurt him as much as she could, so had accused him of sexually assaulting her daughter by a former marriage. Doc claimed that his wife had talked her daughter into testifying against him in order to get him sent to prison and ruin his medical career. I never knew whether he was telling the truth or not. Many of the guys in prison claimed to be the victims of false accusations, especially when a sex crime was involved. Child molesters were at the bottom of the social ladder in the prison, and most inmates would have nothing to do with them. Doc said I was the only prisoner to whom he had confided his story.

Doc poured a cup of coffee for me and one for himself.

"I've been wanting to talk to you," he said slowly. "I haven't had much of a chance to speak to you alone."

"Go ahead," I replied, my curiosity aroused.

"I've walked by your cell a couple of times and noticed you reading the Bible," Doc said. "Maybe you would like

54

to join a Bible-study group."

"I don't know," I said. I still wanted to get straightened out inside. I knew that I needed to make some drastic changes in my life, but I was still shaken by my experience with the prison chaplain.

Before I realized what I was doing, I was pouring out my story to Doc. Surprisingly, he seemed to understand my feelings about God and the emptiness I felt in my life. He nodded his head in agreement occasionally, and looked as if he really wanted to help me.

"I'm glad you're reading your Bible and wanting to find the truth," he said as I finished. "Keep it up, because we don't have much time left."

"What do you mean by that?" I was curious!

"By our calculation, the world should end some time in the next six years."

"You mean Jesus is coming back in six years?" I asked.

"No, Jesus has already returned. He came in 1914," Doc said. "However, the second presence of Jesus is invisible, in spirit. We figure that around six years from now the present system of things will end, and the battle of Armageddon will take place."

I had to admit that this was news to me! I had never heard anything like it before.

"What church do you belong to?" I asked.

"I'm a member of the Jehovah's Witnesses."

"I guess I don't know anything about them," I said. "But if Jesus has already come back, and the world is going to end in six years, then I want to know more about it."

"That's wonderful!" Doc was jubilant as he poured himself another cup of coffee. "We can start you on an individual course of Bible study, and you can also attend our group Bible study on Saturday mornings."

He went on to explain that he could not attend the Bible study because he had been "disfellowshipped" for a year when he was sent to prison. During that year he was not allowed to represent the Jehovah's Witnesses in any way and could not even engage in conversation with another Witness. I did not understand all of this, but I told him I was willing to be introduced to another inmate who was a Jehovah's Witness in good standing.

Mr. Goldstein suddenly appeared in the doorway. "All right, fellows," he began, "I know you like coffee, and I know you enjoy talking, but—"

"OK, OK," I interrupted. "We're going."

"You must realize," Mr. Goldstein continued, "that you have a responsibility to . . . ." He reminded me of one of my old school teachers back in Detroit.

His voice trailed off as I turned and left the room.

Mr. Goldstein didn't like for us to turn our backs on him and walk away, but I enjoyed antagonizing him. Yet I really couldn't understand why I felt this way; I wanted to do what was right, and still I had a terrible resentment of authority.

As I sat down at my desk, I was conscious of being really excited about something for the first time since I had been a prisoner. I had been wishing for someone to study the Bible with me, but I had about given up hope of finding anyone.

Since I didn't know anything about the Jehovah's Witnesses, I began to observe the activities of the prisoners who belonged to this group. For the first time, I realized that they read their Bibles every day during the lunch hour, in the prison yard where everyone could see them. They didn't appear to be disturbed by the ridicule this practice brought them. After reading their Bibles for awhile, they would start witnessing to other prisoners in the yard. Their courage gave me the utmost respect for them, and I could hardly wait for the Bible study on Saturday morning.

A few days after our conversation, Doc came by my cell after supper and asked if I would like to meet Vern, the unofficial leader of the Jehovah's Witness group in San Quentin. He explained that Vern led the individual studies and also led group studies in the yard whenever possible.

I jumped at the chance, and we went together to the television area on the main floor. Doc led me to a fellow who appeared to be just a few years older than I, even though his hair was nearly white. He introduced us and explained briefly that I wanted to join the Bible-study group. Then he left, after telling me that Vern would take care of me from there on.

As Doc turned and walked away, I remembered that he was not allowed to associate with other Witnesses, or even to address them except on important business.

Vern was very friendly, and seemed pleased that I wanted to study with them.

"You'll understand a little more about Doc and our system later on," he explained. "Right now, it may seem rather unfair for him to be disfellowshipped—but it's only temporary; he can be reinstated after a year. In this way we try to protect our members from those who turn away from the faith."

Vern then introduced me to two other Witnesses— Tony, a young Mexican, and Heflin, an older fellow who had been studying with the Witnesses for about fifteen years.

After attending the first Bible study in the educational building, I looked forward to Saturday mornings. For an hour, I got away from the prison population. Mr. Stormer, the overseer of the Kingdom Hall in nearby San Francisco, came out to the prison to conduct the study. Vern explained that the overseer is the leader of a congregation, much like that of a part-time pastor. He is not salaried, however, and preaching and visitation duties are shared by other members of the congregation.

Studying with the Witnesses also brought me several new friends, and true friends were hard to find inside the prison walls. I soon became a zealous witness to the "truths" I was learning, and I even managed to win one convert.

A few weeks after our first meeting, Vern asked me if I would like to move into his cell so that we could spend more time studying the Bible. His cell partner had moved to another cell the day before. I immediately requested the transfer and within two days I had moved in with Vern.

A few nights later, lying on my bunk, I began thinking about the events of the past month. The guard walked by and shone his flashlight into the cell, taking the count. A few cells away, an inmate was snoring heavily.

"Hey, Vern," I whispered, "are you awake?"

"Yes."

"Say, I've been thinking about something," I said hesitantly.

"What's that?"

"Well, I've been wondering if it would be possible for me to be baptized."

"You know, I've been wondering the same thing, Larry. We would have to check with Mr. Stormer and see what he says. If he's willing, we would still have to get the approval of the prison authorities. That might be hard to do."

I thought about it some more after Vern went to sleep.

Being baptized would make me a full-fledged Witness, and I would then be entitled to lead other Witnesses in prayer. Their rules stipulated that only baptized believers could lead in prayer. I always enjoyed leading, no matter what the activity was, but the idea of leading a prayer group was especially appealing.

"Almost like being a preacher," I thought.

My thoughts were interrupted by the footsteps of the guard returning for the next cell count. After he had passed by, the only sounds were the steady dripping of water in the sink and Vern's heavy breathing. Soon I drifted off to sleep.

The next day was Saturday, and after the morning Bible study Vern presented our request to Mr. Stormer. Somewhat to my surprise, he gave his consent to my being baptized and promised that he would try to get permission from the assistant warden.

To my great disappointment, I learned the next week that Mr. Stormer's request had been turned down. The Jehovah's Witnesses baptize only by immersion, and the authorities felt that there would be too great a security risk in allowing an inmate to leave the prison in order to be baptized. Furthermore, they knew that if they allowed one prisoner to do so, others would demand the same privilege—perhaps from motives that had nothing to do with repentance.

Vern and I talked it over some more and worked out a plan for getting me baptized without the authorities' permission. We presented our proposition to Mr. Stormer the next Saturday.

"It's all right with me," he replied after some hesitation. "But I don't want you fellows to do anything that would bring reproach on us. Something like this could even stop us from coming into the prison for our weekly

Bible study."

Although we promised Mr. Stormer that we would be very careful, the plan we had worked out could have gotten us into serious trouble. Al, the inmate whom I had recently led into the Jehovah's Witnesses, was a trusty who came around in the mornings and unlocked the doors to the cells. He had agreed to unlock our cell early the next morning, even though he knew he was risking his status as a trusty.

Vern and I slept in our pants and socks that night, and it seemed that I had hardly fallen asleep when I heard the key turn in the lock. "OK," Al whispered, "come on out! The bull just went around the corner."

We jumped out of bed and slipped our shoes on. "You're not nervous, are you?" I asked Vern.

"A little," he admitted. "You know what this means if we get caught, don't you?"

"Yes, but we're not going to get caught," I said confidently. "Come on—look happy!"

In answer, Vern shook his head—but he left the cell with me, and the three of us walked down the catwalk and around the corner of the cell block, then down the steps to the shower area. Next to the showers was a large mop tank, big enough for a person to fit into. We started filling this with water, trying to be as casual as possible.

Al hissed a warning. "The bull's coming!" he said, pointing to the end of the cell block. We looked up and saw the guard heading our way.

"Act like you're trusties getting ready to mop," Al instructed us in a stage whisper.

Vern and I fumbled with a couple of mops. We were shaking—I was anyway! The guard drew near, glanced at us and passed by. We continued to play with the mops until he disappeared around the corner.

"Whew!" Vern said.

"Yeah," I agreed, "whew!"

In a few minutes—which seemed more like hours—the tank was almost filled, and Vern turned the water off.

"Let's go!" he said.

Quickly I stepped into the tank and sat down. Vern grabbed me.

"I baptize you," he said, pushing me under the water, "in the name of the Father, the Son, and the Holy Spirit."

Coming up out of the water as quickly as I could, I stepped out of the tank and unplugged the stopper at the same time. The baptism had been so hurried that I wasn't sure it had "taken." The only thing I felt was wet.

"Come on, Larry! Hurry!" Vern said, running toward the stairs.

I wasn't far behind him, and we reached our cell in safety, without being observed. The trail of dripping water would dry before the guard made his next round. Closing the door softly behind us, I looked at Vern and smiled.

"I wonder," I panted, "what the guard will think if he goes back to the shower room and hears the water running out of the tank?"

"Maybe he'll think someone was baptized!" was Vern's retort.

Chapter

6

A Further Search

It was early Saturday morning, and the cells had not yet been unlocked for breakfast. The chill wind from San Francisco Bay seemed to come right into the cell block and into my cell. I snuggled down under the covers and lay thinking about the time since I had been baptized in the mop tank.

For the past several months, I had enjoyed being a part of the Jehovah's Witnesses. It felt good to be part of a group that had a genuine concern for both body and soul. In the loneliness of a prison, I had found companionship and human beings I could trust. Trust was not to be given lightly in San Quentin.

I thought about the Bible lesson I was to conduct this morning, and my heart beat a little faster. Each of the Witnesses was required to take a turn presenting a lesson. I had studied hard and looked forward to the time with nervous eagerness.

Hearing the click and clatter as the guards unlocked the cells, I jumped out of bed and slapped cold water on my face. I hurried to breakfast, but I was so anxious to get back to my cell to go over the lesson again that I hardly tasted my French toast. I had gone out of my way to select an unusual subject: the significance of the Tetragrammaton, the four Hebrew consonants for God's name. Wow! I had wanted something challenging and interesting, and I was sure I had both.

Many of the inmates remained in their cells on Saturday morning, choosing to skip breakfast for the extra sleep. And yet there were still hundreds of cons in the mess hall, and there was a low hum of conversation, but most were intent only on gobbling their food so they could hit the yard to feed the gulls and visit together.

Leaving the mess hall, I set out across the upper yard. There was a loud, piercing whistle, and I stopped dead in my tracks. The hair on the back of my neck was quivering. I knew the shrill whistle was the dreaded signal that a guard on the catwalk above our heads had spotted some unauthorized activity and all movement was to stop instantly. My eyes moved in my head. I wanted to see what was going on, but I was afraid to move a muscle for fear I might be shot. There were several inmates in the yard, but I couldn't make out what the trouble was. A shot rang out, the sheet-metal of the protecting roof amplifying the sound. I could hear several men shouting, and then four bulls came tearing into the yard, heading for the central area where the domino tables were. Carefully I turned my head. Now I could see what had happened. There had been a fight at the domino tables, and at the sound of the guard's warning shot, both men had quit and they were standing there motionless, their hands raised in surrender. They looked like a still picture for a cops-and-robbers movie.

The four guards escorted the two men toward the maximum security unit located in the center of the prison. I breathed a little easier, and headed back to my cell to go over my Bible lesson one more time.

At ten o'clock I attended the Bible study, and my diligence paid off. My lesson went over big. Vern, Heflin, and several of the others commented on what a good job I had done. Even Mr. Stormer, usually impassive, nodded his approval several times during the presentation.

"The significance of the Tetragrammaton," Vern said, carefully writing the words on a slip of paper. "I'm going to tell my mother about that the next time I write home!"

"That was a good lesson. No kidding," Heflin said.

"Very interesting," Mr. Stormer said, nodding. "Very interesting."

I was walking on air.

The hours and days and weeks slipped by. I would often glance at the clock in the furniture factory office with the dread realization that my life was passing by, wasted behind the prison walls. I saw my life as an hour glass, time trickling away, from future to past, from hope to utter despair.

After work I would return to my cell looking for a letter, some word from home, wanting to keep in touch with the outside world. The only world a prisoner knows is the world in which he lives daily, and the world outside soon becomes something abstract. One of the cruelest aspects of prison life was standing at one vantage point just off the upper yard where we could see automobiles winding up and down a highway. It seemed at times as though this scene were especially staged to mock the inhabitants of San Quentin. I would stare at the moving cars, and anger would begin to boil somewhere deep inside me. I wanted desperately to be free—free to roam, free to do as I pleased whenever I pleased. Then something—or Someone—would turn the heat down a little. The boiling would stop. Instead of anger there would be only sadness and the pain of regret.

I continued to look for letters, but they seldom came. Since there were no visits and few letters, I began to read more of the literature supplied by Mr. Stormer and the Kingdom Hall he oversaw in San Francisco. But the more I read, the more I challenged what was being taught in the publications. There were obviously a few unexplainable inconsistencies between their teachings and the teachings in the Bible.

Several things were bothering me. The sect claimed that Jesus had already returned and set up His kingdom in 1914; that it was spiritual and invisible. This did not concur with the words of the angels in Acts 1:10:

And while they were gazing into heaven as he went, behold, two men stood by them in white robes, and said, 'Men of Galilee, why do you stand looking into heaven? This Jesus, who was taken up from you into heaven, will come in the same way as you saw him go into heaven.'

If He was to come in the same manner, then reason would dictate that His return would necessitate His being visible to His disciples as He had been at His ascension.

Another matter of concern to me was the very negative attitude of the organization toward all of the mainline denominations. With great acrimony, they wrote and spoke of them with contempt, blasting the clergy at every available opportunity, and branding all ministers as allies with Satan himself! Their sectarian attitude bothered me. All through the four Gospels Jesus kept pounding away at the idea of love: "Love one another," "Love your enemies." Their hatred didn't seem Christian to me. Furthermore, it didn't take long for me to realize that they also bordered on claiming infallibility for their leaders. Indeed, they taught that none of Christendom would inherit eternal life outside the fold of the Jehovah's Witnesses.

But the most glaring error seemed to be their insistence that *Jesus Christ was none other than the archangel Michael!* While I did not understand all the implications of such a position, I realized that Jesus Christ could not be both the Son of God and the archangel Michael. Hebrews 1:5 says: "For to what angel did God ever say, 'Thou art my Son, today I have begotten thee'? Or again, 'I will be to him a father, and he shall be to me a son'?"

Prompted by these lingering questions, I began to read all of the theological books I could find in the prison library. I soon recognized, as I had suspected, that the Witnesses' position was a blatant departure from orthodoxy. I was beginning to wonder what I had gotten myself into.

One night Vern and I were trying to have what he called a "Bible study" in our cell. Actually, Vern was reading aloud from one of the Watchtower books, and we discussed each paragraph after he read it.

I was listening to Vern with one ear, and with the other I was trying to follow the television program drifting up to us from the television area directly below our cell. During a commercial I heard Vern say, " . . . so the only thing we are permitted to take is a blood substitute. We're not permitted to have blood transfusions."

"Wait a minute," I interrupted. "Say that again."

"I said, and I repeat, that we are not allowed to have blood tranfusions. We're required to take a blood substitute."

"How come?" I said, thinking of several people I had known who would have died if they hadn't had blood transfusions.

"That's what the Bible commands us to do, Larry. And

if you're going to be a good Jehovah's Witness you've got to conform to the rules and regulations."

"Aw, come off it!" I said. "You know as well as I do they didn't even have any such things as blood transfusions when the Bible was written!"

Vern ignored my protest and went on to explain again that neither Jehovah's Witnesses nor their children are permitted to have blood transfusions.

"We would rather obey God than listen to man's advice," Vern told me.

Again I was prompted to study even harder to find the true answers to these many questions. But the more I studied, the more I began to realize that this religion I had become involved in was not the religion of the New Testament. It was not the same as Christianity. For awhile though I continued to meet with the group for weekly Bible study. Then I gave it up. I kept on reading the Bible in my cell every night, trying my best to understand it but not having much success. One night Vern walked into the cell and found me poring over the King James Bible.

"You know you're not supposed to be reading the King James, don't you?" he said bitingly. "I told you very clearly that the only Bible we are allowed to read is the New World Translation."

"Yeah, I heard something like that," I answered, and kept on reading.

Vern laid the palm of his hand over the page I was reading so I couldn't see it.

"You know, Larry," he said, trembling with anger, but trying hard to control it, "you might as well move out of this cell if you're not going to study with us. One of the other guys could move in."

"If you want to move out, go ahead," I said, "but

me—I'm staying put!"

From that time on, Vern and I talked only when necessary. For awhile I kept on reading the Bible, but I
couldn't understand it, so finally I decided to give up. I
returned it to the library.

Chapter
7

One Day at a Time

During the summer of 1964 the alternates from the United States Olympic boxing team were scheduled to come to San Quentin to hold matches with several of the inmate boxers. A makeshift ring was constructed in the lower yard where hundreds of inmates would gather to watch the fights.

With nothing better to do on that festive Saturday morning, I ambled down to the lower yard to watch the fights along with the other prisoners. The Jehovah's Witnesses had stopped associating with me when I quit attending their meetings, and now that I was no longer a part of their "Bible studies" I had more time on my hands—too much time, for I was lonely.

The yard had been shrouded by fog earlier in the day, but now it was lifting slowly, and the events were about to begin. The first fighters were being introduced when there was a commotion in the large crowd. My heart jumped, and I craned my neck to see where the trouble was. Guards were rushing into the throng. A moment later they brought out an inmate who was clutching his abdomen. There was blood on his hands, and his face was twisted in pain. While he had been watching the fights attentively another inmate had sidled up to him and stabbed him.

A wave of uneasiness swept through the yard, and for the remainder of the bouts most of us watched with less than full attention. We kept a wary eye on the men near us, ready at any moment to ward off an unprovoked attack.

Marie Killilea, who wrote the book *Karen*, has observed that we are a nation of conformists. I believe this is a correct observation and one that is standard until one reaches a prison like San Quentin. It is here that one lives, or attempts to live, in the midst of a group of nonconformists—murderers, rapists, thieves, racists—never knowing what to expect next, never knowing which breath could very well be the last.

There were guys like Crazy Frank, a Mexican prisoner who must have been in San Quentin since the year One. He walked about talking to himself and shadow boxing, sometimes talking to a cement wall. We were afraid of him because we knew that he was off his rocker. We knew that he could snap at any moment and plunge a shiv into an unsuspecting inmate's back. Then there were the white bigots who thought black people were sub-human with no rights whatsoever, and there were the black bigots who claimed that the white man was the devil. There were the warring Mexican factions, split inside the prison walls because their hometowns were feuding with each other down in Mexico. There was just no peace for anyone. The only time I felt really safe was when I was locked in my cell.

To make time go faster, I began visiting the library. Up until then I had read only westerns, but one day I picked up Ernest Hemingway's *A Farewell to Arms*. That was the dynamite that opened me up to good literature. I found a whole new world between the covers of good books. I discovered that I could escape to sun-drenched Spain with Hemingway, or mentally don a cloak and sword to relive French history with Dumas. Sometimes when I was shaving I would be mulling over the incidents in a book, and suddenly I would notice myself in the mirror, and I would think, "Is this me, Larry Howland?" I marveled that I would have any interest in the kind of books my English teachers had tried futilely to stuff down my throat.

One night I was in my cell reading *The Sun Also Rises* when the aroma of freshly grilled cheese sandwiches reached me. My mouth started watering. I laid the book aside, checked my pocket for cigarettes, and headed for Sammy Kellog's cell on the fifth tier. I didn't like Sammy Kellog, and usually I tried to avoid him, but I couldn't resist his grilled-cheese sandwiches.

"Boy, does that smell good!" I said, handing Sammy a pack of cigarettes in exchange for a sandwich.

"You can smell them clear down there?" Sammy grunted. "Hey, Charlie, stoke up!"

Charlie, Sammy's cell-mate, was standing outside the cell, furiously puffing on a cigarette to try to cover up the odor of melting cheese and butter on toasted bread. Now he put a second cigarette into his mouth and puffed on both of them simultaneously.

"Surely," I thought as I left them, "they must realize the guards know there are contraband hot-plates in various cells throughout the block."

Sammy Kellog was one of the toughest, meanest cons in San Quentin, but he was ingenious. Many of the prisoners were not only ingenious but also resourceful and industrious. It required an incredible effort to develop an enterprise such as Sammy had put together. The hot plate had to be constructed and smuggled into the cell, and

71

once there it had to be concealed so the guards who casually walked by the cells observing inmate behavior would not see it. I was convinced that many of the guards would avoid going by the cells, wanting to make life a little more pleasant. However, if a guard actually saw such activity in the cell, he would have to report it, and of course these things could not be hidden from the searches without notice, almost always when the inmates were not in their cells. If a hot-plate or a weapon were found, the owners simply had to accept the consequences. This was one of the business hazards that entrepreneurs such as Sammy faced, one of the risks of the "business" world inside a prison.

In addition to this, they had to obtain bread, cheese, and butter in fairly large quantities. This could be arranged by bribing a kitchen employee, but there was still a great risk in smuggling the material out under their shirts, a little at a time. But then the risks also had dividends: for each sandwich sold, the seller took in a pack of cigarettes, the unofficial prison currency. Because of the low salary in the prison, most of the men smoked tobacco purchased in bulk quantity, and then rolled their own cigarettes. It was mainly those who had their own businesses who smoked the real thing. The rest of us would buy cigarettes, not to smoke, but to barter with. This tobacco currency would purchase items such as sandwiches, pay off gambling debts, or even pay to have another con killed.

As I continued to frequent the library, I was increasingly amazed by the number of men who visited there to study the law books hour after hour. These were the "jailhouse lawyers,"—men who, for a fee of perhaps several cartons of cigarettes, would examine a man's case and prepare legal briefs or papers to be filed in the local county court. Some of them were experts at finding legal loopholes that just might mean freedom for their clients.

It would surprise many of those "on the outside" to realize that many inmates are intelligent and capable of being productive and constructive individuals. The annual art show at San Quentin displayed the artistic talents of many inmates serving life terms for murder, kidnapping, or some other reprehensible offense.

Prisoners were proud of the accomplishments of San Quentin cons. They boasted about Carl Chessman and Bill Sands. Chessman spent twelve years on death row before dying in the gas chamber. He had the highest IQ of the inmates in the prison, and while a prisoner on death row, he wrote a book entitled *Cell 2455 Death Row*. It is said that the authorities would not give him permission to write the book, but that he smuggled his manuscript out on *carbon paper!* His attorney would carry an attache case in with fresh carbon paper to exchange with Chessman for those containing the manuscript. The officials, when searching the attorney's possessions, paid no heed to the carbon paper.

Bill Sands has published two books, *My Shadow Ran Fast* and *The Seventh Step,* and is the creator of the Seven Steps program, an organization devoted to helping other convicts find eventual freedom, not only from the prison, but from the life of crime which has enslaved them. As I learned all of these things, I began to see that there may be a ray of hope after all. But I still could not shake the deep, hazy feeling that the only real, genuine hope was to be found in the Person of Jesus Christ.

One Saturday as I was leaving the library to return to my cell, I heard Doc calling me. "Hey, Larry! Where have you been? I've been looking all over for you." Doc was the only Jehovah's Witness who was still friendly toward me.

"What's up?" I never knew from day to day what one of my friends might involve me in.

"You've got a visitor. They've been calling your name for the last half hour."

"A visitor?" My heart leaped. I couldn't believe it. "Who would come to see me?" Even as I asked the rhetorical question of Doc, the loudspeaker called, "Howland, 82008, you have a visitor; report to the main gate."

A strong breeze was blowing papers and debris across the ground as I hurried to the main gate. The excitement was almost unbearable for this was my first visitor. Who could it be? My heart was beating wildly with anticipation. I wished it were Mom, but I knew that was impossible. She and my stepfather were living in Indiana now, and I knew that was too far for her to come. Could it be my sister Norma? Maybe Aunt Thelma? The only person I knew in California was my dad, and I was sure that he would not come all the way from Los Angeles to see me. I finally reached the main gate, took everything out of my pockets and waited impatiently while a guard searched me thoroughly. Then I was escorted into the visiting room.

I looked around the room, and then I saw him. *It was my father.* He was standing on the other side of the long table that had a partition reaching all the way to the floor to prevent forbidden exchanges between prisoners and visitors. He looked very neat and handsome standing there, and it flashed into my mind, "He's still a lady-killer!"

We stood looking at one another, not saying a word. Finally he broke the silence.

"How are they treating you?" he asked.

"OK," I said. I was unexpectedly overcome by emotion. In spite of everything, I wanted to love my dad, and I wanted him to love me. In spite of all the years of hating, I wanted to reach out to him, not just physically, but to really be a son to him, and to have him really be my father.

We sat down, the partition between us. It had been a long time since we had seen each other, and our last visit had been brief.

"What are you doing up here?" I asked. My voice was husky.

"I've moved to San Jose so I would be close enough to visit you." He was looking me straight in the eye, but even as he spoke I knew he was lying. He had always lied. It was something he couldn't help—being a compulsive liar. And now I smelled the alcohol on his breath.

"Dad," I said. My throat was tightening, and I could hardly speak. "Have you been drinking?"

His dark eyes twinkled, and he looked amused. He shrugged his left shoulder and said, "Oh, I had a few on the way over here. Nothing to worry about."

I looked at him dumbly. I couldn't think of anything to say.

"Have you seen your mother?" he asked.

So that was it. Ever since their divorce, even though he also had remarried, he had never given up hope of getting Mom back.

"No, she hasn't been out," I said. "I guess she can't afford the trip. But anyway, I don't expect her to come all the way out here to see me."

"Does she write?" he persisted.

"Once in awhile."

"Look, Larry, I want you to do something for me," he said. He was putting on his cozy, buddy-buddy act, and I knew that if we had both been on the same side of the partition his hand would be on my shoulder. "Larry, I want you to write and tell your mother that I need to see her. Tell her if she will come out here I'll pay her plane fare. I wrote to her three or four times, but she won't answer any of my letters."

Sudden anger and pain filled me like a big balloon. I wanted to cry. I thought I would burst if I couldn't cry! I wished miserably that our family could be back in Fairborn, Ohio—only without the beatings and without the anger and the unfaithfulness. I wished that my parents had never been divorced. I wished that I were still a child, running to meet my daddy as he came home from work. I wished I were a little boy and that he would be nice to me.

"Maybe your mother and I could get together again, Larry, if she came out. She still loves me, Larry. She loves me, and she needs me, Son. Promise me that you will write to her. And tell her I'll pay her fare."

As he continued to talk on and on about his desire to be reunited with Mom, I began to realize that we were both prisoners. I wasn't sure whose prison was worse: my San Quentin, or his bondage to alcohol and self-delusion.

Finally the guard announced that the visit was over, and I stood up to leave. Dad stood up too, his eyes still looking into mine in that friendly, persuasive way.

"So-long," I said.

"Write your mother, Larry. She'll be glad to hear from you. Tell her I want to see her. And tell her I'll pay the fare."

His voice seemed to follow me all the way back to my cell, and my cell was a welcome shelter that day. I was glad to be back in it. I lay on my cot, and with my head buried under my pillow I cried a lifetime of tears.

Chapter
8

Farewell to San Quentin

Two weeks after my father's visit, Doc, Eddie, and I were in the lower yard enjoying the sunshine when Kincaid came hurrying up to us.

"Wendy's in trouble again!" he panted.

"What's the matter?" Doc asked.

"I was up in the gym, and some guy told me that five guys cornered Wendy in the back room." Kincaid didn't have to explain any further. Such incidents had occurred before. Several guys would corner one inmate and force him to submit to a homosexual act.

By the time we got to the gym it was all over. There was normally no guard stationed in the back of the gym, but one happened to walk through on a routine check just as Wendy was actually about to give in. When the guard came through the door, Wendy walked out as though nothing had happened. If he had informed on the group, he wouldn't have lived through the week.

Wendy was so badly frightened by this incident that, instead of coming to us for help, he found a knife and cut himself on the arm. Then he went to the captain of the guard and told him that another inmate had cut him. At his own request, he was locked in South Block for protective custody.

Once an inmate was locked in protective custody, he almost had to stay there until he was released from prison. If he asked to be released from protective custody and be put back in the regular cell block, the other inmates would consider him a coward and would run all over him.

I went back down to the lower yard and sat alone in the bleachers by the baseball diamond. The sun was hot and reflected off the metal backstop in front of me. I suddenly felt a threatening loneliness now that Wendy was in the lock-up. In prison, where friends are few, the absence of one of them is felt sharply. Wendy had been frightened since the day he walked into San Quentin, but so had everybody else. Some were able to take the pressure, and some weren't. Wendy couldn't take it, and I was sorry. I never saw Wendy again.

Shortly after Wendy left us, I noticed that Eddie was drifting away from our group. Finally I asked him what the trouble was.

"Nothing, Man! Just leave me alone," he said. He refused to look at me as he spoke. He would look past me, or glance over my head, or watch his own hands, but he just wouldn't look me in the eye anymore.

"If something's wrong, tell me," I persisted. Eddie had been such a clown before, always gregarious, always looking for some way to make us laugh.

Eddie shifted from one foot to the other.

"I gotta go, Man," he said. "I gotta go now. I'll see you later." And he walked off, not even glancing back. What was the matter with the guy?

Slim, a big fellow from Oklahoma, had been watching us. He ambled up to me now, rolling a cigarette and running the tip of his tongue along the edge of the paper.

78

"Didn't you hear about Eddie?" he drawled. "Eddie's been turned out."

His words hit me like a punch in the stomach. I thought I was going to throw up.

"I don't believe that!" I said.

Slim held the finished cigarette in one hand and took a makeshift toothpick out of his pocket with the other. He toyed with one of his teeth for a few seconds before he answered me.

"Well, I'm just telling you," he said. "I ain't saying you got to believe it."

But it was true. Word quickly got around, and it was confirmed that Eddie was indeed the homosexual partner of a prisoner in North Block.

A few days later at the end of the lunch hour, I was walking through the lower yard to get to the gate leading into the furniture factory. Just as I approached a group of guys sitting around talking, another inmate came up to them. When he got in front of them, he suddenly pulled a long knife out of his pants. He held the knife in his right hand and it was held so tightly I could see the white of his knuckles as he brought up his hand.

"Look out!" one of the guys screamed.

The con with the knife lunged at a fellow sitting in the middle of the group. He did not have time to get out of the way, and his eyes were wide with terror as he raised his arms to try to ward off the attack. The knife came down on his back, but fortunately for him, the homemade shiv did not penetrate, but merely glanced off his backbone. The guard standing watch in the tower above hadn't even noticed what had happened.

I quickly appraised the situation. If I stopped walking, or began walking faster, I would draw attention either way. I kept on walking as if I hadn't noticed either.

As the victim of the attack tried to run, his attacker grabbed him by the arm, whirling him around. He hit him with his fist and knocked him to the ground. I could see that if I kept on walking I would be right between them.

I took a deep breath and kept walking. The attacker once again started for his victim on the ground and had the knife raised for another blow when I walked in between them. As I did, the terrified victim on the ground jumped up and ran to the guard at the gate of the furniture factory. A few minutes later they were escorting him away to be locked up in protective custody.

I walked on into the furniture factory and went to work, dimly aware that God had again intervened to save my life and had helped me to survive in this corner of hell.

Two days later, I received word that the parole board wanted to see me again. With mingled curiosity, fear, and hope, I made myself as presentable as possible and reported to them.

When I walked into the interview room, the chairman of the parole board, a heavyset man with a dark complexion, addressed me in a deep voice. "Mr. Howland, we are going to be very brief and to the point. We're wondering if you have reconsidered your previous position. Are you ready to sign the waivers now?"

The joy I felt at hearing those words surprised even me.

"Yes, sir!" I replied. "I'd sign anything to get out of this place."

The chairman informed me that I would be released to Georgia since they had first put out a warrant for my arrest. The release date was set for October 1, 1965, two months away.

I was overjoyed—grinning from ear to ear as I headed back to my cell.

As I reached the entrance to North Block I came face to

face with Sam Kellog of the grilled-cheese-sandwich business. He was a former heavyweight fighter and a mean cuss. Except when the aroma of his sandwiches got too much for me, I avoided him like the plague.

"Hey, Howland," he said, stepping toward me, blocking my way. "What did the parole board tell you?"

"They're going to let me go, Sammy!" I said. My policy was to avoid Sammy when I could, but to be very nice to him when I couldn't.

"That's nice, Baby," he said, and the way he said it curled my hair. Eddie flashed into my mind, and my feet started to sweat and freeze both at the same time.

"You know what, Howland?" he said. "I'm gonna turn you out before you leave this place. You come up to my cell at seven sharp tonight. You got that?"

I knew he meant it, and he knew that I knew he meant it. He stepped aside now, and let me pass. I was so scared I thought I might have a heart attack and almost wished I would.

Vern was in the cell, shaving and getting ready for supper. We hadn't spoken to each other for weeks —except when absolutely necessary.

"You look sick," he said. "Are you OK?"

"I'm OK," I said. I was too sick to talk.

At supper that night I couldn't eat. My stomach was one big knot. What was I going to do? Doc and Kincaid and I were eating together, and I considered sharing my problem with them, but decided against it. If it came to a fight I knew I didn't stand a chance against Sammy, but I didn't want to drag my best friends into it. Anyway, I didn't want to fight. With my release from San Quentin in sight, I didn't want to mess up my good behavior record. But I could never, never submit to being turned out. If it meant that or die, I'd rather die.

By the time supper was over my mind was made up. I knew exactly what I was going to do, but I didn't dare imagine the consequences.

"God, help me," I said.

Seven o'clock came too soon. Sammy was propped on his bunk reading a murder mystery when I walked up to his cell. He looked up and grinned like a gargoyle.

As I looked at Sammy in the dim light from the tier, I realized this could be the last day of my life. These could be my last words.

"You can wipe that grin off your face, Sammy. I've got news for you. I don't want you to ever say another word to me. You just keep off my back. You got that?"

Sammy looked stunned. He looked as if he couldn't believe it. With added courage, I turned my back on him in a gesture of contempt and walked away. I knew he might knife me, but for those few seconds I was as cool as ice. I didn't even look back, but just kept walking. Sammy didn't follow me.

As the day for my release drew near, I became more and more anxious. I asked Mr. Goldstein to check with the assistant warden, to find out for sure that the release was going through. He reported back that no word had been received from Georgia yet, so I sweat it out for three more days. On the morning of the fourth day I found Mr. Goldstein waiting for me at the door when I arrived at work.

"Good morning, Larry," he said. "I want to talk with you for a minute."

I looked hard at his face to guess whether the news was good or bad, but I couldn't tell. He had called me by my first name. That was unusual. He usually called us by our last names. I weighed the possible significance of this, and wished that he would stop shuffling the papers on his desk and get down to business. Finally he pulled the chair out from behind his desk, sat down in it and motioned me into the chair across from him. Then he started playing with a pencil.

"On the way home last night, Larry," he said, "I just happened to see Mr. Murdock." He paused. I realized he was enjoying my suspense.

"He asked me to give you a message."

"What's that?" My voice was sharp with apprehension.

"A telegram came from Georgia yesterday. They don't want you." Mr. Goldstein smiled broadly as he gave me this news.

"Are you sure?" I could hardly believe it.

"Yes, I'm sure—but don't get too happy. The prison has notified Michigan to pick you up."

I didn't hear anything else he said. For the first time since the judge had passed sentence on me, I began to feel that my prison term might actually have an ending as well as a beginning. I was already starting to dream about the day when I would discard my prison garb and walk the streets again—a free man!

Chapter
9

"God Loves You and I Love You"

The day was dull for October—the day I was to have my first glimpse of the outside world in almost two years. By 11:00 A.M. I had packed my few belongings and exchanged happy-sad farewells with Doc and Kincaid. There was no way to get word to Wendy that I was leaving, and Eddie still avoided us.

I sat on the bench outside the visiting room, waiting to be picked up by the sheriff from Michigan. Guards and trusties were passing back and forth as they went about their duties, but I don't think I even saw them. I was too excited about getting out. But underlying my joy was a cold fear. What would happen when I got back to Michigan? Would I be sentenced to forty years in prison? To ten years? I felt I couldn't bear even one more year of confinement.

For the first time in many weeks I really opened up to God. Isn't that crazy? When my life had been in real danger I scarcely gave Him a nod, but now as I was sitting in the safety of the main gate my thoughts turned to Him. It felt as though my bunched-up soul was melting and spreading out and out in a smooth, thin layer, like water in a calm, shallow lake. It was a beautiful feeling.

"God, please help me out of this mess," I prayed. It seemed like a selfish and awkward prayer to go with such a beautiful feeling.

The sheriff finally arrived. He was a short, stocky man with a businesslike approach. Once again shackles were put on my hands and feet, and I was taken out to his car to begin the journey to Michigan where my career in crime had started. It was a three-day trip. We ate in restaurants and slept in county jails. The sheriff and I got along well, and after the first day he removed my handcuffs and shackles. I was grateful.

When we arrived in Lapeer, Michigan, I was placed in the Lapeer County jail to await trial for armed robbery.

The next day I was taken to the courthouse to be arraigned. Before the judge arrived in the courtroom I glanced toward the door. Standing there, looking anxiously into the room was a dark, heavy-set woman with heavy features. My heart skipped about ten beats.

"Aunt Thelma!" I cried.

"Larry!" she exclaimed. She came quickly into the room and embraced me.

Aunt Thelma is my mother's sister. I've always felt close to her because my parents left me with her one time when they went on vacation. To me she was a kind of North Star, somebody who stayed in one place and could always be relied on.

"What in the world are you doing here?" I asked her.

"Why, I came to see you! I'm going to consult a lawyer and see if I can't get you out of here on bail."

Aunt Thelma had driven eighty-five miles to see me, and she wanted to help me! I was so touched I had to fight back the tears. I had thought that no one cared about me anymore. Now that she was with me, the cold knot of loneliness and fear inside me relaxed just a little, and a faint ray of hope penetrated the deep gloom of my spirit.

Before we had a chance to talk any more, the deputy tapped me on the shoulder. "The judge is here and wants to see you now."

After my arraignment, I was allowed to visit with Aunt Thelma for half an hour in the visitors' room of the jail before being taken back to my cell. She informed me that my mother and sisters, though anxious about me, were doing quite well.

Before she left, she promised to come back and said she would also send her minister to see me. After my experience with the chaplain at San Quentin, I wasn't sure I wanted to see a preacher—but I was too grateful to Aunt Thelma to hurt her feelings by refusing to see him.

I spent the next few weeks locked in a twelve-foot by twelve-foot cell with three other inmates: Junior, a middle-aged fellow locked up for non-payment of alimony; Duke, a nineteen-year-old who was serving a ninety-day sentence for vandalism; and Joe, an alcoholic about fifty years old who was in jail more than he was out.

After the relative freedom of San Quentin, where I had been confined to my cell only at night, I found it rough to be locked up in a small cell with the same three guys twenty-four hours a day. Our only reading matter was some books and magazines brought by my cellmates' visitors, and we had no access to a television set or a radio.

To pass the time away, we played poker for hours on end, using matches for chips. The stakes were the next morning's breakfast which consisted of two small doughnuts. The food ration in that prison was small and we were constantly hungry, so these were high stakes. After going without breakfast for two weeks at one stretch, I decided the life of a gambler wasn't for me!

The combination of confinement, boredom, and hunger often wore our tempers thin, and some of our poker games could hardly be called friendly. One evening Junior threw in the last of his matches and announced somewhat petulantly, "If I lose this hand, I'm out."

"Aw, quit complaining, Man! You've won for the last four days," was Duke's reply.

"Why don't you both shut up and just play?" Both the words and the tone of my voice clearly expressed my growing irritation.

A quarrel was averted by Joe's urgent "SSHH! I hear someone coming! I think it's the sergeant."

"Now, how can you tell it's the sergeant?" Duke asked sarcastically.

"I've been here so many times, I know his footsteps like the footsteps of my own mother." Joe's attempt at humor struck me as rather pathetic.

"Hide the matches," Junior broke in. "They might take the cards away if they find out what we're doing."

Duke whisked the matches into his pocket just in time. A moment later the key turned in the lock, and the sergeant stuck his head in the door.

"Howland," he said, "you have a visitor."

As I followed the sergeant out of the cell, Junior called after me, "See if you can get us something to read." I didn't bother to answer him. I was too busy wondering who the visitor was, and why I was allowed to see him after visiting hours.

I didn't recognize the well-dressed man sitting in the visitor's room with a small briefcase on the floor beside him. As I came in, he stood up and shook hands with me.

"Good evening, Mr. Howland, my name is John Peters.

I'm the local overseer of the Jehovah's Witnesses. I heard about your coming here and wanted to see you. In fact, I brought you one of our Bibles—the New World Translation, published by the Watchtower Bible and Tract Society." Reaching into his briefcase, he brought out a large Bible and handed it to me. Then he told me that the local congregation of Jehovah's Witnesses was praying for me and hoped I would receive my release very soon. I listened politely but made little response. After a few minutes Mr. Peters prayed with me and then left.

As the sergeant escorted me back to my cell, I thought back over some of the things Mr. Peters had said, and over my experience as a Jehovah's Witness at San Quentin. I had a sour feeling I can't quite express. Before we arrived at my cell door, I had made a decision.

"Sarge, I have a request."

"What's that?" The sergeant had always been friendly to me and seemed willing to help any way he could.

"I don't want to see any of the Jehovah's Witnesses again. Would you tell them that for me if they come back?"

He put his hand on my shoulder. "Sure, Larry. And remember, the sheriff and the guys here are all for you."

"Thanks, Sarge," I replied. He unlocked the door to my cell, and I rejoined my cellmates. By that time it was too late to finish our poker game, and the next morning's doughnuts were divided four ways.

The days went by slowly as I awaited my trial. The sergeant kept me informed of the proceedings, and he told me that my aunt was unable to make my bail. As I awaited the trial date, I almost memorized the magazines and books that we had in the cell, but I didn't even open the Bible Mr. Peters had brought me.

About three weeks after Mr. Peter's visit, I had another evening visitor.

"Say," I told the guard as I followed him down the hall, "the sergeant promised he wouldn't let the Jehovah's Witnesses visit me anymore. What's the deal?"

"It's not a Jehovah's Witness," was the guard's laconic reply.

Again I was taken to the visitor's room. The stranger who stood up to greet me radiated warmth. He gave me a big smile and a hearty handshake.

"Hi, Larry! My name is Pastor Zuber. I'm your Aunt Thelma's minister. She asked me to come and see you."

I sat down, and for a few minutes we talked about Aunt Thelma, my mother and my sisters. I felt comfortable with Mr. Zuber—a little the way I used to feel with Grandpa Howland when I was a little kid and would sit on the floor next to his chair.

"Larry, have you ever met the Lord Jesus as your Savior?" Pastor Zuber asked gently.

"Yeah, I guess so," I said. The comfortable feeling was replaced by a sense of embarrassment which I didn't understand. Why should I be embarrassed to hear a preacher speak of Jesus?

"Do you mind if I read you some scriptures?" he asked.

"No, that's all right," I said. I was trying to be polite, but for the next fifteen minutes I suffered real anguish. I wanted desperately to get out of that room. I wanted back in my cell!

Finally Mr. Zuber stood up to leave, and I breathed a sigh of relief. The heat was off, and I relaxed. Oh the Lord is smart! He knows us so well! He knows just when our guard is down and He can come in. Right then, when I was breathing easy again, and my embarrassment had subsided, Mr. Zuber put his arm around me and said very simply, "God loves you, Larry, and I love you." And I knew it was true. For the first time in my life *I knew God loved me*. I had read it in the Bible a hundred times, but it had never sunk in. And now I knew it was true. I was so astonished I couldn't say a word. Mr. Zuber handed me a pocket-sized New Testament and said goodbye, and I took the book and watched him leave, but I couldn't say a word.

As I followed the guard back to my cell confusion set in. The glory of the moment had gotten mixed up with another feeling that I couldn't name. I felt dirty. I felt as though I needed a good bath. I didn't understand it.

When I walked into the cell Duke looked up from his cards.

"Who was it?"

"Just a preacher," I said. For an instant I was tempted to make a dirty joke about it, to say, "He even put his arm around me and told me he loved me." But I couldn't. Something deep inside me wouldn't let me.

Duke made some remark, and I laughed with him, but inside I wasn't laughing at all. I was troubled in a deep, painful way I didn't understand.

I knew God loved me. I would never doubt that again. But what about the other things the preacher had said? Was it true that I had to believe in Jesus in order to be saved? That if I didn't accept Jesus as my Savior I would go to hell? The Jehovah's Witnesses had told me that all I had to do was dedicate myself to Jehovah, and I had done that in San Quentin. I had even risked my neck to be baptized. Wasn't that enough? I was thoroughly confused.

As I walked into the cell, I saw the day's mail had finally been delivered. I picked up the one remaining letter, wondering who had sent it. I studied the return address. It was from Doc, but it had been mailed from Colorado, and the return address was Denver! I tore the envelope open and read:

Dear Larry;

Surprise! The parole board called me in unexpectedly, and they gave me an immediate release. I am in Denver right now where I've been promised a job working in the office for a pharmaceutical firm . . . ."

I was glad for Doc, genuinely glad, but it came to my mind that if Michigan returned me to San Quentin my old friends there would all be gone. Doc had been released, and Kincaid was soon to be released. Wendy was in protective custody. Eddie was a queen. If they sent me back I would be alone. I would have no one.

"Hey, Larry!" Joe yelled. "Wanna play a game of poker?"

"No, Man! Shut up and leave me alone," I yelled back. I wasn't as polite to Joe as I had been to Pastor Zuber.

"OK, OK. You don't need to be so touchy," he said.

I sat down on my bunk and read the rest of Doc's letter. As I finished it and put it down, I noticed the pocket New Testament the preacher had given me. It was a King James translation. Should I read it? The Jehovah's Witnesses said that the only Bible a Christian could trust was the New World Translation, and that other translations were of the devil.

But why should I believe what they told me? I had tried their religion, and had found it empty and lifeless. Undecided, yet wanting some comfort from the loneliness, I flipped through the pages of the Testament Mr. Zuber had given me. Suddenly a verse caught my eye, and my whole attention. Propping myself up in my bunk, I began reading at John 3:16 and read until the lights went off.

For the first time, the Bible was beginning to make sense to me. The scriptures pertaining to salvation were underlined in red, and as I read them I came under the clear conviction that if I died at that very moment I would go to hell. Jesus had given His life to save me from my sins, but I had not accepted the salvation which He offered me.

After the lights were turned out, I lay on my bunk and all of my past sins and wickedness seemed to flash before me. I sat up and groped for Mr. Zuber's New Testament. Almost of its own accord, it opened to the passage that had aroused my interest when I first picked it up. In the dim light I read, *"For God so loved the world that he gave his only begotten Son, that whosoever believeth in him should not perish, but have everlasting life."*

My fellow prisoners were asleep now. Reassured by their heavy breathing, I began to pray in a whisper, "O Lord Jesus, I want to believe in You. I don't want to be a sinner any more. O please, dear Jesus, forgive me for my sins. Save me! *Please save me!*"

Suddenly I was oblivious to everything around me. My cell and my soul seemed to fill with warmth and light as Jesus came into my heart. In the radiance of His love, the cold, heavy burden of anger, sin, guilt, hate and fear simply melted away and I knew that Jesus had saved me and given me His everlasting life. Joy unspeakable welled up in me.

"Thank You, Jesus!" I prayed. "Thank You! Thank You! Oh, thank You!" I said it over and over again.

Life was no longer dark; things no longer seemed hopeless. If God loved me enough to let His only begotten Son be put to death for my sins, He certainly loved me enough to take an interest in the circumstances of my life. And if

He had the power to raise Jesus from death, He could certainly control those circumstances in my life! Why should I be afraid?

Committing my spirit and my future into the hands of my loving, heavenly Father, I drifted off into a sweet and peaceful sleep.

Chapter
10

One Answer to Two Prayers

It was a beautiful day, even from inside a cell! I wakened just as the sun was rising, and I could see it through the narrow, barred window. Soon the trusty came with the doughnuts, and even the doughnuts were fresh. In a way it was just another day, and yet for me it was so different, so new. The whole world seemed as though it had been washed and pressed and splashed with a high-class brand of shaving lotion. I pondered what had happened to me the night before. I turned it over and over in my mind, relishing every small detail. When my cellmates wakened I told them all about it, and they listened with respect. Nobody kidded me. Nobody said, "You're off your rocker."

I decided the first thing to do was to write a letter to Judge Churchill, my trial judge, and let him know what had taken place. I wrote him a ten-page letter, and gave it to Sarge to have delivered for me. I had no idea what the judge's reaction would be until I stood before him for sentencing during the first week of January, 1966.

"Mr. Howland," Judge Churchill said as he looked at me sternly, "I believe what you said in the letter you wrote to me. I've listened to many different stories, but I believe you are sincere. You well know that you are at the crossroads of your life. You have a choice about what to do with your life, and that choice has to be made now. I have decided to sentence you to one to ten years in prison. I'm giving you a ten-year maximum, and you can believe that if you ever stand before me again I'll make sure you do all of that ten years. But I'm giving a one-year minimum, recommending the earliest possible release, and I'm also giving you credit for the three months you have spent here in the county jail."

My heart was beating fast, and I felt mixed reactions to his words. I hated the prospect of going back to prison, but I was thankful for the recommendation of Judge Churchill. I was determined to keep my commitment to the Lord, and I was expecting an early release.

Two days later I was transported to Jackson by Sheriff Parks. Once again, I walked into a prison, but this time the feeling was different; I knew it was only temporary, and that I would have a constant Companion. Jesus would be my Cellmate.

I was processed and sent to Camp Waterloo, a minimum-security prison camp, designed for prisoners who could be trusted. Mr. Zuber and Aunt Thelma came to see me often. They always brought me books and encouraged me to study the Bible.

Even before I talked with the parole board I knew that I would be released. When Judge Churchill had recommended the earliest possible release, I knew God was moving and it was time for me to pack.

One happy day six months after my sentencing, about twenty other fellows and I were taken to the basement where we were given civilian clothes. Then we were ushered into a large room where visitors were waiting. A tall, thin officer stood to one side calling each of us by name. As he called our names we responded, and then we were free to leave.

"Larry Howland," the guard called. As soon as he called my name I saw two people rise from their seats and head in my direction. They were Mom and Mr. Zuber! I forced back the tears. There's a myth, you know, that convicts don't cry!

"Mom!" I held out my arms and she flew into them. "You came all the way from Dayton!"

"Larry!" She was crying and hugging me with all her strength.

I turned to Mr. Zuber and shook his hand. He smiled warmly at me, and I thanked God for this man who had cared enough to come to a jail and tell me about Jesus Christ.

On the ride to Taylor I sat back and enjoyed the scenery. It was June, springtime in Michigan, and everything was fresh and clean and sweet-smelling.

"Aunt Thelma wants you to stay with her," Mom said.

"That's great," I said. I could almost taste Aunt Thelma's chocolate pie with the graham cracker crust. She would have one in the refrigerator waiting for me, and I knew it.

"Know what I'm going to do first?" I said, and before Mom could answer I went on, "I'm going to paint her swing for her. Does she still have the swing on the back porch? Is she going to have a little garden this year? I can spade it for her if she is. Have the storm windows been taken down yet? I could take them down and put up the screens for her." I was drunk with the joy of freedom.

Mom had to go back to Dayton the next day. I was sorry to see her go, but she looked younger and happier than she used to, so I figured she was happy. She had lost weight and bleached her hair, so I guessed she was feeling younger too.

I quickly settled into the routine of civilian life, living with Aunt Thelma and working for a man in her church who owned several service stations. I worked in one of them for eighty-five dollars a week, but within two weeks he promoted me to manager and raised my salary to 125 dollars a week. I felt like a king.

I began attending church with Aunt Thelma. We went to the Taylor Wesleyan Church on Van Born Road, and on my second Sunday in Taylor she said, "There's somebody I want you to meet."

We were coming out of the sanctuary, and as I turned to see whom she was talking about my eyes met the most gorgeous deep green eyes I had ever seen in my life. Several inches south of the eyes was the prettiest mouth I ever saw—and the sweetest smile.

" . . . Bonnie Thiede," Aunt Thelma was saying when I got my brain in focus again. "She teaches third grade, but she's planning to go to graduate school to become a social worker."

I'm not saying it was love at first sight, but I don't know what else to call it. I got it into my head that for the sake of my cause Aunt Thelma ought to invite her over to the house for ice-cream and cake. After I had coaxed and pleaded for three days Aunt Thelma could take no more.

"You're driving me crazy!" she said. "Call Bonnie yourself and ask her for a date!"

"Couldn't you call for me?" I pleaded. I was as scared as a kid in junior high. Aunt Thelma picked up a book and pretended she was going to throw it at me.

"She's at a meeting at the church right now. Call her there," she ordered.

It took a lot more nerve to make that phone call than it

had taken to pull a robbery back in the old days. This was sure a new Larry Howland! I wasn't certain where the old one had gone, but I was glad he was among the missing.

I dialed the number and heard the phone at the church ring twice. Then Pastor Zuber answered.

"Mr. Zuber, Sir," I stammered, "this is Larry Howland. May I please speak to Bonnie Thiede?"

"Sure, Larry, just a minute!" Obviously Pastor Zuber was totally unaware of what I was suffering.

"Bonnie?" I said, still suffering.

Aunt Thelma was watching me over the top of her book. *"Ask her!"* she ordered in a stage whisper.

I was acting like a kid, and I knew it. But I hadn't dated a girl for years, and in the back of my mind was the cold, gnawing fear that she would turn me down. However, she didn't turn me down. We went bowling the next evening, and she was so nice to me, so sweet that I forgot my fears for the time being.

I couldn't sleep that night for thinking about her. I went to work the next morning, still thinking about her. In fact, I just could not get my mind off her, so I decided to call her. I figured nine o'clock in the morning would be a fine time to call a girl I had just dated one time!

As it turned out, I called her six times. She was doing the wash, and I was busy with customers, so I would hang up and wait on them and then call her back again. We made a date for that night to go to a concert in the park. I'm not very enthusiastic about symphony music, but I don't think I heard it anyway. I was too busy just looking at Bonnie and thinking how wonderful she was. I had been praying for a Christian wife, and something seemed to be telling me that Bonnie was the one God had chosen. I know now it was the Holy Spirit telling me, but I didn't realize it then.

However there was a cloud on my clear horizon. Sooner or later I would have to tell her that I was an ex-convict. I would have to tell her about the crimes I had committed and the time I had spent in prison. How would she take it? Would it put an end to our romance before it even got off the ground?

The concert was over, and I took her home. The porch light had burned out and hadn't been replaced yet, so we sat on the porch swing and talked. Sometimes I was only pretending to hear what she was saying because I was praying for the courage to tell her about myself.

"Bonnie," I said, "I want to tell you something."

"What is it?"

The chains holding the swing were squeaking in a gentle rhythm, and a neighbor's cat was twisting itself around my legs.

"Bonnie," I said again, "I've got to tell you something awfully important."

"Well, go ahead," she said.

"I don't know how to say it. It's a hard thing to say."

"Well, you can try," she said.

"But if I tell you, maybe you won't want to date me anymore."

"Don't be silly," she said. "Go ahead and tell me."

"I'm an ex-convict."

The swing stopped for just a second. I don't know whether her foot stopped it or mine.

"Tell me about it," she said. We were swinging again in the same easy rhythm.

I told her briefly, quickly. She didn't say anything for a long, long time. I was praying silently, "Lord, if you don't want me to date her anymore it's OK. But Lord, I think I'll die!"

"If you don't want to date me anymore, it's OK," I said

nervously. "I'll understand."

"No, I don't feel that way," she said, moving a little closer to me. "You're not in trouble anymore. You're a Christian now. The past doesn't make any difference. *You are a Christian, aren't you?*"

"Yes," I said. "Yes, thank God I am." I could scarcely speak. Gratitude, love, relief, joy—all were crowding my heart.

The weeks flew by while I waited for a decent period of time to pass before asking her to marry me. I prayed. I asked her. She prayed. And she said, "Yes."

Bonnie had her bachelor's degree in education from Marion College in Marion, Indiana, and had planned to start working for her master's in sociology, but when we decided to get married she changed her mind.

"I'll keep teaching, and you start working for your bachelor's degree," she said. When I hesitated she said, "But it's the sensible thing to do. After we are married I promise to be a good, submissive wife—the very model, Darling—but I will never let you rest until you at least try to get into college!"

We were married in March in the Taylor Wesleyan Church. Bonnie talked me into memorizing our wedding vows so we could repeat them to each other instead of saying them after Mr. Zuber.

The organ was beginning to play when she whispered to me, "Honey, there is something I have not told you that I think you ought to know."

I recalled my own painful confession to her that night when we were sitting on the front porch of her rooming house.

"What is it, my baby?" I said.

"Not long before I met you I started praying for a Christian husband."

"Baby, you know what?" I said. "I was praying for a Christian wife before I met you."

A few minutes later the most beautiful girl in the world married the happiest guy in the world, and we both said our memorized vows without a hitch. Praise the Lord.

Bonnie and I moved into the used mobile home we had bought, along with Pierre, a French poodle we received as a wedding present. The trailer was ten-foot by fifty-foot, but to me it seemed like a mansion after being confined to a jail cell for almost three years.

The next Sunday God taught me a lesson that I was to remember many times. Just before leaving for church on Sunday morning, I picked up the checkbook to write out our tithe check.

"Look at this," I said, showing the check balance to Bonnie. "We only have twelve dollars in the bank. If we pay our tithe of eleven dollars, that will only leave us one dollar in the bank. Maybe we shouldn't pay it this week."

"No, I think we should pay it," Bonnie responded. "The Lord will take care of us."

"Yes, but do you think we should be foolish?" I was thinking this thing could be carried too far.

"No," Bonnie said simply. "I think we should trust Him."

I had a lot of confidence in Bonnie and her faith, so I wrote out the check. She had learned what it was to live by faith when she had gone to Marion College. Her parents were not able to finance her education, so the entire burden had fallen on her. She had to buy her own clothes, pay for her tuition, her room, her boarding, her meals —everything. Many times, she did not know where the next dime was going to come from to pay for doing her laundry or to meet some other need. She worked as many hours as she possibly could and still carried a full load in

101

school. In fact, many nights she fell asleep while kneeling in prayer beside her bed.

One time she needed a third history book, and there was no money to pay for it. The book cost twelve dollars and she only had seven. She prayed and trusted the Lord, having no one she could turn to for the money. That afternoon she received a call to work a few hours cleaning up a house in town. She thankfully accepted the opportunity to work, realizing that this would partially pay for the much-needed history book. In her regular job in the college cafeteria, she earned eighty cents an hour. She figured if she worked three hours cleaning house, that would give her another $2.40 to add to the seven dollars and would leave only $2.60 for her to earn before she would have enough for her history book. That afternoon she went to work and, to her delight, she ended up working four hours instead of three. As she finished, the lady of the house came to her. "Let's see," she said. "You worked four hours. Would $5.00 be enough?"

It was exactly enough to pay for her textbook! She stood on the street corner after she left the house, crying and praising the Lord for His goodness.

As I thought of experiences such as this happening in Bonnie's life, I was ashamed for not wanting to write the tithe check. I wanted to have the same faith Bonnie had, to really believe in and trust in God.

The next day I came home and Bonnie was waiting for me at the door.

"Guess what we got in the mail?" she asked excitedly.

"Probably something good since you're so excited."

"It's a check from the Internal Revenue Service. We made a mistake on our income tax and we got back over a hundred dollar refund."

"But I didn't think we had any money coming back," I said.

"Well, how is that for the Lord taking care of us?"

"Great," I said, "just great!" After all, if God could influence the Internal Revenue Service, who was I to lack faith?

Chapter
11

School Days

A week after the tithing episode I sent for an application to Marion College. To a lot of people I guess it would sound crazy to say that I was really dying to get back to school. I had hated school! I hated it so much I dropped out on my seventeenth birthday and joined the army, and now I could hardly wait to hit the books again. Sometimes my eagerness worried me—I was afraid I was being selfish in keeping Bonnie from getting her master's degree.

"Honey, don't you understand?" Bonnie said, giving me the old bear hug. "I've got *you* now. What do I want with another degree! And besides, I want you to have a real chance to develop that marvelous brain that God gave you." Let me tell you, that woman sure knows how to make a guy feel ten feet tall.

Several days after we mailed the application, Bonnie and I went to a revival service at the Taylor Wesleyan Church. Here's another thing: would you believe it if I told you I got a real thrill out of being there that night? Me. Old Mr. Rough Stuff. I just sat there and thought, "This can't be old Larry Howland. No way, Man!" The choir was singing all those hymns I used to think were so corny, and there was a big basket of white flowers sitting up in front of the pulpit. I remember when I would have made fun of those flowers; I would have said they looked like a funeral. But now they looked beautiful. I was wishing I could smell them.

There was a little boy—a real little fellow—sitting next to me, and I felt as if I just loved that kid. I'd never even seen him before! He had a purple crayon, and he was using it to color a picture of an Easter bunny in a coloring book.

While I was watching the little kid I noticed something was happening to me. A sweet peace had come over me, and I felt again as though I were being enveloped in a soft, sheer scarf.

The evangelist's voice broke through to me, and I heard him saying something about his alma mater, a school called John Wesley College in Owosso, Michigan.

I caught my breath. Even though I heard no audible voice, I knew the Holy Spirit was speaking to me.

"That is where I want you to apply," the Holy Spirit said. *"You are going to school there."*

Wow! It was like an electric shock. God had never communicated to me so clearly before. I knew without any doubt that this was what God wanted.

"Do you have a piece of paper?" I whispered to Bonnie. She looked at me quizzically, then opened her purse and drew out a notepad and pencil.

"The Holy Spirit just spoke to me, and told me we are going to John Wesley College," I wrote.

Bonnie read the note slowly, her mouth dropping open. Then she smiled like an angel and reached for my hand. We sat there rejoicing, feeling the sweet presence of the Holy Spirit.

We did not know anything about John Wesley College,

but I sent in my application, trusting God to take care of the details. At the same time, we sent a letter for Bonnie to the Owosso School District, applying for a teaching position. Then we settled down to the sweet torture of waiting for replies. Two weeks passed, and the assistant superintendent of schools phoned Bonnie from Owosso, offering her a job teaching third grade. Another month passed before I heard from the college. Then one night when I came home from work Bonnie met me at the door, threw her arms around me and squealed, "You made it, Honey! You've been accepted!"

We both rejoiced and thanked Jesus once again for shaping our future.

The next few months were busy ones as we prepared to move to Owosso, eighty-five miles north. We made arrangements to move our trailer on to the campus, and in August we moved.

School enrollment time was nearing, and Bonnie and I realized we did not have the tuition money we needed to cover the first semester. We took our problem to God and asked Him to solve it for us. His answer was not long in coming.

We both had cars since we had each owned one before we were married. Bonnie had an old Ford Falcon, and I had a newer Karmann Ghia. We decided to try to sell the Karmann Ghia.

Mr. Clinebell, the used car dealer, came up a couple of days later to look over the car. He was a large, sober man with a little round, red nose.

"Well, let's see now," he said as he slowly thumbed through his blue book. He hummed a little tune as he looked.

Bonnie and I stood anxiously waiting to see what he would give us for the car. We owed twelve hundred dollars on it, and needed four hundred to be able to pay the tuition. That meant we needed sixteen hundred for the car.

A robin chirped merrily on a branch above Mr. Clinebell, as he stood looking at the Karman Ghia, and then studied the book again. I hoped I would be as happy as that robin when I heard his offer.

Mr. Clinebell cleared his throat and walked over to the car. Even the car looked as if it were anxious to know how much it was worth.

"Well, folks," he said, "about the best I can do is eleven hundred dollars."

"*What?*" I almost choked. "I still owe twelve hundred dollars on it."

"You have to take the body into consideration, Mr. Howland. It needs some extensive body work." I knew he was right. There was no use arguing with him.

"Well, thanks for coming anyway, Mr. Clinebell." I turned and started to walk dejectedly into the house with Bonnie.

"Wait a minute," Mr. Clinebell said. "How much will you take for that Falcon?"

I looked at Bonnie, and she looked as surprised as I felt. We had not even thought of selling Bonnie's car. It also needed a lot of work, and we did not figure we could even get what it was worth.

"I don't know," I replied. "What would you give for it?"

"Is it paid for?" he asked.

"Yes, we paid it off a couple of months ago."

"I'll tell you what," Mr. Clinebell said. "I'll give you four hundred dollars even, just the way it sits."

"It's a deal," I said, awed and humbled at the way God wonderfully provided every need.

Two weeks later I walked into the business office and

paid the four hundred dollars tuition in cash. **Praise the Lord.**

I went to my first classes with a sense of anticipation mingled with dread. It had been seven years since I had been in school, while most of the students were just out of high school. I also wondered how an ex-convict was going to fit into the picture. Only a few of the faculty were aware of my situation, and I was advised that I should not make my past known to the other students, as it was felt that this would be a time of adjustment, and it would be much easier if I could be just another student. I decided to follow the advice of the faculty. However, I did confide in one student, Richard Strait. He also was older than the other students and had received his call to preach after he had married and begun raising a family. It helped to have someone I was free to talk with openly.

For my first semester, I signed up for psychology, English, speech, religion, and Greek. Richard and I had a couple of classes together, and another older student, Jack Gladding, was also in one of our classes. We felt a little more comfortable among the younger students, knowing we had the company of one another. We met often for coffee and would discuss our classes and talk about our Christian experience.

Jack had been called to preach when he was forty years old. He lived on a farm and did construction work. Coming to college was even more of an adjustment for him than it was for Richard and me. In addition to our times of coffee and sharing, we would take our burdens about the school work to the Lord in prayer. During one such visit, Jack was telling us about the church he attended. He was, unofficially, the pastor's assistant and this gave him the opportunity to preach occasionally.

"How would you like to come and preach for us some

Sunday, Larry?"

"Praise the Lord!" I responded. "I'll come this Sunday if you want!"

"Wait a minute," Jack said, "I'll have to clear it with the pastor first."

Two days later Jack told me that he had talked with his pastor, and he had liked the idea of having a student come to preach. The date was set for three weeks later. Those were very slow weeks, as I was anxious to preach and share from God's Word.

"What do you think I should preach on?" I asked Bonnie one night.

She smiled at my obvious enthusiasm.

"Preach on whatever you feel the Lord would have you preach on," she answered, and gave me a quick kiss.

I walked into my makeshift study. Our trailer had had two bedrooms in it when we bought it, so I had converted the smaller room into a study. We purchased a desk, and packed it, a couch, and a bookcase into that tiny bedroom. There was hardly room to breathe but that is where I spent several long hours studying and praying over my very first sermon. The Lord led me to preach on Matthew 24. I felt the urgency of His second coming, and felt that in these last days people should be aware that Jesus is going to return.

Bonnie and I finished supper about 5:30 on Friday evening, two days before I was scheduled to preach. Bonnie went out and got the paper off the porch. "No, put that down," I told her. "I have something for you to do."

"What's that? You didn't mention any plans for tonight."

"I don't have any plans except we're going to church."

"Church? Where?"

"Right here. At home. I'm going to preach my sermon to

you and I want to know what you think of it."

Bonnie sat down on the couch and I put a chair in front of her. On top of the chair I put a little stand to use as a lectern. The chair and the stand together were about the same height as I imagined the pulpit would be. And then I preached my sermon—all twenty-five minutes of it —while Bonnie listened patiently. My sermon finished, I waited for her reaction.

"Well?" I asked.

"Well, what?"

"How was it?"

Bonnie thought for a moment. "Well, it was different," she said finally.

"What do you mean different? How was it different?"

"It's just that I've never heard anyone quote so many statistics on earthquakes and famines and wars in one sermon before!"

"So who asked you anyway?" I said, folding my Bible and diving back into my study to make some last-minute revisions. I could hear Bonnie laughing in the living room as I got busy again.

Richard and his wife, Beverly, sang together occasionally, so I asked them to come along and sing for the congregation. After a little coaxing, they agreed. I also asked Tom Molby and his wife, Pat, to sing. Tom had been a folk singer before his conversion, and he hoped eventually to have a ministry in music for the Lord.

We arrived at the Crystal Wesleyan Church about 9:00 A. M., one hour before Sunday school and two hours before church. It was a small white frame building that needed a little work. Jack had told us the congregation was small but loved the Lord and loved preachers. It was a good place to get my feet wet, but I was nervous anyway. I kept looking at my watch and checking to make sure it hadn't stopped.

At last we were in the church, and the service was underway. The preliminary part of the service seemed so long that I wondered if maybe they had forgotten I was there to preach. Maybe somebody had made a mistake in the little mimeographed program and had skipped the sermon. I was afraid to check my bulletin for fear somebody would think I was bored, so I just sat there, my heart pounding and sweat rolling down between my shoulderblades.

My turn finally did come. I stumbled on my way to the pulpit, but at least I didn't fall on my face. I breathed a silent prayer to the Lord—a silent wail that must have made the angels cry! Then I took a deep breath and plunged in. I must have rattled off that sermon at machine-gun speed because it was all over in ten minutes. I glanced at Bonnie for reassurance, and she was beaming. Thank You, Jesus!

I enjoyed school, but sometimes it was rough. There were times when I felt I just didn't have the mental capacity to get through. In fact, if it had not been for Bonnie I'm pretty sure I would have quit school long before graduation. It had always been difficult for me to finish anything I started, but Bonnie helped me to persist. Now that I was a Christian, I really wanted to do a good job, but I needed Bonnie to keep me going, to assure me that in Christ I could do anything.

More than once I thanked the Lord for His divine guidance in sending us to Owosso. All of the professors under whom I studied at John Wesley stressed the importance of living a Christian life, no matter what field we planned to enter after graduation. There was one professor in particular who won a very special place in my heart. She was Bertha Kienbaum, my Greek professor. She had started teaching at Owosso Bible College in 1931, before the name had been changed to John Wesley, and during leaves of absence the Lord had used her in various places as a missionary and teacher. Once she served as principal of a Bible Institute in South Africa. Her entire life had been given to educating young men and women for the ministry and various endeavors in life. Many young men, when they got out into the ministry and faced the hardships and trials that sometimes accompany the pastorate, could look back to the times of being in Miss Kienbaum's classroom and thank the Lord for the spiritual guidance they had been given there.

Tom Molby was also in my Greek class, so we would get together to study in the evenings, trying to master what is really a quite difficult language. I had flunked Spanish in high school, so I felt that if the Lord wanted me to get through that course He was going to have to give me some special tutoring! When I found out there were *twenty-four* different ways to write the article "the" I threw up my hands and said, "Lord, help me!" And He did. Sometimes He helped me directly, but sometimes it was through dear old Miss Kienbaum. She was so patient with us. When Tom or I would be stumped on the conjugation of a verb or trying to figure out what case a word was by its ending we would sometimes use that as an excuse to phone Miss Kienbaum, and she would work with us on the phone until all of our questions were answered.

On one occasion I invited Miss Kienbaum to come and hear me preach at Dick Gleason's church in Ovid. It was my third sermon, and counting Bonnie, myself, Miss Kienbaum, a neighbor lady and her daughter who went along with us, there were eight people present at the service! No matter, I preached as though the church were full, thankful for the opportunity.

In class the following Tuesday, Miss Kienbaum announced that she had gone to hear me preach. "Larry has a very interesting sermon illustration I would like for him to share with the rest of you," she said.

I shared my illustration, and I was so proud! Proud and grateful. It really meant a lot to me to have her treat me with such gentle, loving respect. It healed a lot of wounds.

Teachers like Miss Kienbaum made me feel capable of learning, but it was Bonnie who kept me at it, and she was as thrilled as I was when the first semester ended, and I learned that I had earned B plus in Greek.

Chapter
12

The Sound of a
Rushing Mighty Wind

The March wind was howling through the tops of the bare trees and our trailer was trembling ominously. The campus of John Wesley College is situated on a hill, and many of the trailers in the small trailer park jut out precariously over the edge, supported only by cement blocks. But ours was not one of them, and on that particular night I was praising the Lord that ours was stationed across the street, partially protected from the wind by the laundry building on one side of us and a large oak tree on the other. I wasn't worrying about myself, but I was worried about Bonnie.

Bonnie had left earlier in the evening to attend a meeting at Northgate Wesleyan Church. I had finished studying and was reading *Mr. Jones, Meet the Master,* by Peter Marshall. As another fierce gust rocked the trailer, I winced, wishing Bonnie were safe at home. I glanced at the clock for the tenth time in fifteen minutes and then forced myself to concentrate on my book.

Still a baby in the Christian faith, I felt challenged by some Christians who seemed to have so much more power than I. The questions kept nagging me: Why did some have more zeal and dedication than I? Why did some have more penetrating insight? What factor —analyzing it logically—made the difference? It especially troubled me that I had never made any converts.

I laid aside Marshall's book and took up my Bible, turning to the book of Acts. As I read it I was struck by the dramatic change in Peter. Throughout the Gospels I always seemed to identify with Peter; he was a man I could understand. Like myself in the old days, he was argumentative, impetuous and violent. Can you imagine anybody having the gall to grab Jesus by the arm and lead Him aside and rebuke Him? Peter did it. And I would be willing to bet Peter was the one who tried to chase the little kids away the day Jesus blessed them. The night of the Last Supper he argued with the Lord when the Lord wanted to wash his feet. A few hours later he took a sword and chopped off a fellow's ear. That same night he told people he didn't even know who Jesus was, and he was cursing when he said it. Yes, whenever I read about the "old Peter" I also remembered the "old Larry."

But the "new Peter," the Peter in the book of Acts was a total mystery to me. The Holy Spirit came, and *wham!* Instead of telling people he had never heard of Jesus and instead of hiding himself in a locked room, he was standing out on a street corner preaching, and his sermon was so powerful that three thousand listeners immediately accepted Jesus as their Savior! *Three thousand people!* I knew something very real had to have happened to him to cause such a change. I wished it could happen to me.

Again I read the second chapter of Acts, and this time I was impressed by the unusual things that happened at Pentecost. The scene was vivid. I could hear the sound of the rushing mighty wind. I could almost see the bright tongues of fire falling upon the 120 disciples gathered in the locked room. But speaking in tongues? That was beyond my imagination.

"I wish it could happen to me," I thought.

As I was pondering the mysteries of Pentecost, the front door flew open and Bonnie shouted, "Hi, Honey! I'm home!"

I rushed to the living room and hugged her tight.

"I'm so glad you're back! Isn't the wind wild! I'll bet you were scared half to death."

"I did pray a couple of times," she said, smiling. She was always so cool, so trusting of the Lord. Even my wife seemed to have more spiritual power than I had.

We sat down in the living room with a bowl of walnuts and a nutcracker, and while we cracked the nuts and chewed on the meats I shared what I had been thinking.

"I wish it could happen to me," I said in conclusion.

"It can," Bonnie said simply. "I was baptized in the Holy Spirit when I was a freshman in college."

"You were!" My head was reeling. I had thought of the baptism in the Holy Spirit as something that had happened two thousand years ago. To realize it was still happening, and that it had happened to my own wife was staggering.

Bonnie was saved when she was eleven years old, and was the only Christian in her family. As she left home and went off to college, God began to deal with her in her Christian life. He wonderfully used the classrooms and the chapel services to help her mature as a Christian. In fact, it was at Marion College that she first learned that a Christian should pray and read the Bible daily. It seemed that God was continually showing her that He had something more for her.

"When I was a freshman," Bonnie said, "I felt that I had reached a stage of crisis. I felt that I was either going to go forward in the Lord or face a long, spiritual drought. One day in chapel I felt the Holy Spirit was present. After the sermon there was an altar call, so I went up to the altar to pray. All at once I could feel the Lord speaking to me, telling me I was like Thomas—full of doubts and unbelief. He told me that something was missing."

A nutmeat fell on the floor and I picked it up, ready to pop it into my mouth.

"Don't eat that. It's dirty," Bonnie said. "Anyway, that night in the dorm I got down on my knees and confessed my sin of unbelief, and right then God sent His Holy Spirit. I've never been bothered by doubts since then!"

"Well, what do I have to do to get the baptism in the Holy Spirit?" I asked.

"Ask for it."

"Ask whom?"

"God, of course."

"Just that simple?"

"As simple as that."

I began to pray for the Holy Spirit, and for God to change the ineffectiveness I still felt in my life.

A few days later I went to chapel, not realizing that God was going to begin to answer my prayer that day. Chapel services were held on Monday, Wednesday, and Friday, and quite often, guest speakers were invited to come to the college and share with the students. On this morning, the guest speaker was Wesley Smith, author of *Mission Impossible* and *Gateway to Power*. I sat glued to my seat as I listened to a man who had had an encounter with the living God! He told us of his work with teen-agers on the streets of the city of Flint, and of living a life of faith with a complete dependence upon the Lord Jesus Christ. After hearing Wesley Smith, I was really excited for I knew I had heard an unusual man of God. I was even more determined to find the answer I was looking for.

The months passed, and soon the first year of school was over. Bonnie and I talked it over, and we decided I would go to summer school full time so I could graduate in three years instead of the usual four.

In September I was elected president of the College Evangelistic Association, a student organization responsible for carrying the Gospel to the jails, hospitals, and the streets. We were allowed to sponsor one chapel service a year, and we could pick a speaker to come in and represent us. One day, as we were discussing whom we should invite, Wesley Smith came to mind. Most of the officers of the association had heard him speaking in chapel the previous year, and they wanted to hear him again.

I phoned him and asked if he would be willing to come.

"Sure, Brother!" he replied. "I'll be glad to come."

He came a few weeks later, and after the service I talked with him for awhile. He invited me to visit him at his home, so after class one day I hopped into the Karmann Ghia and headed down U.S. 27.

When I arrived at his house, Wes ushered me into the kitchen.

"Come on in, Larry. Mind sitting in the kitchen? I've got the coffee perking here. Sit down now, and tell me what's on your mind." His Bible was lying open at his end of the table so I opened mine too.

"I'm dry," I said. "I don't know what's the matter with me. I pray, but nothing happens. I'm preparing to become a minister of the Gospel, and I've never succeeded in making a single convert."

Wes stirred his coffee and took a sip before he spoke.

"Larry, what you need is to be filled with the Holy Spirit."

I felt as though I had just put my finger into an electric outlet!

Wes turned a few pages of his Bible and began to read about the Holy Spirit. Like Bonnie, he made it sound so simple. Just pray. Ask God to send His Holy Spirit, and He would do it.

"Here's what Jesus says in John 14:14: 'If ye shall ask anything in My name, I will do it!' That's a promise, Larry," Wes said.

"Wes," I said softly. "I want to pray for the Holy Spirit right now."

Wes pushed back his chair. "Good," he said. "Let's get Primrose in on this too." He called his wife, and she joined us in the kitchen. We knelt, and they laid hands on me. As soon as we began to pray, all my cares were suddenly lifted from me. A wonderful joy filled my whole being. We began to laugh and praise God. I had always thought it was customary to weep when receiving the Holy Spirit, but here we were laughing and praying at the same time. My disappointments and discouragements were gone. There was only a precious, heavenly Presence that filled my being and coursed through my whole body. We continued praying, and I soon lost all track of time. It was wonderful; it was marvelous; it was fabulous; it was every adjective I could think of that was good and that would bring praise to God.

"Wes," I suddenly interrupted, "I want to pray for the mighty rushing wind like they had on the day of Pentecost."

"Why do you want to do that, Brother?" Wes asked. "You've already received the Holy Spirit."

"I know," I replied, "but I want to see God work a miracle. He said that whatever we ask in His name, that He would do it. I want the mighty, rushing wind to come."

"If you're going to pray for the mighty, rushing wind

then get out of our kitchen!" Wes said. "You're praying to a mighty, living God who answers prayer. I don't want Him to tear up my house."

I was laughing, but Wes was serious. He believed God enough to know that He could indeed bring the mighty, rushing wind. I jumped up and headed outside.

"Come on, Wes. I'm going outside and pray some more for the mighty, rushing wind," I said.

Wes followed me, and I stood outside and prayed, asking God to perform a miracle.

"You're forgetting one thing," Wes spoke up. "The apostles didn't *receive* a mighty, rushing wind, but they heard the *sound* of the mighty, rushing wind."

"That's right, that's right!" I cried. And then I began to pray even harder. "Dear God," I asked, "are You a liar? You said whatever we ask in Your name, You would do. In the name of Jesus, I pray that You will send the sound of the mighty, rushing wind."

"Listen," Wes said, "I hear something."

I stopped praying and listened, and I heard it too. It was the sound of wind which seemed to come from the north. It wasn't very loud at first, but it rapidly got louder and louder. It rose to a roar, and then slowly began to subside. *God had sent the sound of the rushing, mighty wind!* I had asked for a miracle, and God gave me one! I stood humbled and awed in the Presence of a mighty God.

During the next few days I praised God for an answer to prayer, and yet there was a lingering question in my mind. Why had I not received the gift of tongues as the disciples had on the day of Pentecost? Although Wes patiently taught me on the subject, I began to suspect that even though I said I was open to receiving this or any other gift of the Holy Spirit, I was putting a small barrier between myself and the Holy Spirit.

True to the Wesleyan tradition, the professors at John Wesley College taught that the gift of speaking in tongues was a unique sign given only for the early church. The professors were all sincere men and women of God who felt that such a gift for today was only a demonic counterfeit, and they took great pains to warn us against getting involved with any group or movement that taught such a doctrine.

However, there was one Scripture I could never reconcile with such teaching. In Acts, chapter two, after the Holy Spirit had been poured out on the believers who were obediently seeking the promise, it was necessary for Peter to deliver a sermon explaining this unusual phenomenon. Peter promptly explained that what the world had seen was the fulfillment of the prophecy given by the prophet Joel. His message concluded with an invitation to come to Jesus Christ as Savior. Peter told them in Acts 2:38 to repent and be baptized, and then he said, ". . . and ye shall receive the gift of the Holy Ghost."

In other words, Peter invited them to be saved and to receive the Holy Spirit, just as the disciples had received the Holy Spirit. And then Peter spoke the words that were so exciting to me: "For the promise is unto you, and to your children, and to all that are *afar off*, even as many as the Lord our God shall call" (Acts 2:39).

If I were simply to believe the Bible message, as I had decided I would always do, then I was forced to believe that the promise of the Holy Spirit, including the gift of tongues, was also available and intended for the believers today, in this twentieth century—and that included me.

These thoughts were heavy on my mind when I received an invitation from Wes to travel to Illinois with him for a weekend. He had been invited to speak at a Mennonite church and wanted me to go along and share my testimony with the people. I felt the Holy Spirit was leading in the matter. Wes did not plan to take Primrose on this trip, and Bonnie was going to Niagara Falls with her mother and an aunt, so I felt the Lord must have arranged things so that I could go.

On Saturday evening we rented a hotel room in a small town in Illinois. Trying to save money, we rented one room with two double beds. The room looked like those I had seen in old western movies—the metal-frame beds with sagging springs, a straight-back chair, faded but flowery wallpaper on the walls, and a wooden floor with no carpeting. However, it did have a dim overhead light and a small bathroom with a rusty shower stall. And instead of the classic honky-tonk with swinging doors, there was a fire-hall across the street. A dance for teen-agers was in progress at the hall, and loud laughter, girlish screams and amplified rock and roll music rattled our windows.

Wes was sitting on the chair, reading the Bible aloud, and I was stretched out on the bed. As I listened to him read, I raised my hands and quietly praised God. Wes turned a page and continued reading. I stopped praying and just listened to him. But as I listened, strange words began to creep into my thoughts. They were foreign to me—syllables I was sure I had never heard or read before. Then I felt a sudden urge to speak these strange words. Wes stopped reading and began to pray.

"Thank You, Jesus," he said, "for getting Brother Larry and me here safely."

I began to pray with him, and then I yielded to the promptings of the Holy Spirit. The strange sounding words came out of my mouth. God had given me an unknown tongue!

It was hard to believe it could be so quick and so simple.

Chapter
13

Paul

During the next few days, I could sense that God had touched me with a "power from on high" and that He was going to expect me to put that power to use. Receiving the Holy Spirit had been a wonderful emotional experience, but I knew that God had another purpose in giving me this gift.

The main reason why I had desired the baptism in the Holy Spirit was because I wanted the power to go out and make converts. I wasn't asking to make three thousand on the first day, but I wanted to make as many as the Lord had in mind.

I called Wes and asked him to go with me to witness on the streets of Owosso. I had never done this before, but I knew Wes had been on the streets many times, telling teen-agers about Jesus Christ.

I also called Dick Gleason and invited him to join us. On Friday night Wes, Dick, and I sat in my car getting ready to go out and witness. "Lord Jesus," I prayed, "I've never done anything like this before. I really need Your help. Please lead us to someone who needs You. Amen."

We drove downtown and were approaching a traffic light.

"I feel we should stop and talk with those boys on the corner," Dick said.

Six long-haired boys in bluejeans were standing on the corner smoking and talking boisterously. They reminded me of Tom and me in the old days. They were younger than Tom and I had been, but I could sense the same unchanneled energy boiling in their veins.

"Hello, fellows," Wes said. "Mind if we talk with you for a few minutes?"

"Naw," one of the boys said, "we don't mind, unless you're cops."

"No," Wes replied, "we're preachers, and we came to tell you about Jesus Christ."

I was surprised at the simple and direct way Wes spoke to them. What was even more amazing was that they listened. None of them laughed or turned away. They simply listened, with the same blank expressions my cellmates in the Lapeer County Jail had worn that morning when I told them I had invited Jesus into my heart.

When Wes finished, there was silence. My heart began to move toward these youngsters.

"We love you," I spoke up. "That's why we're here."

These words were the key that unlocked the heart of one of those six kids. His name was Derek, and he looked like a young Viking with his tow hair touching his shoulders.

"I'm on probation," he told us. "Me and some buddies stole a car."

"That's how it starts," I said, remembering my experiences with Tom.

"Well, it wasn't my idea," Derek said. "I was just going along with the guys."

"Yeah," I said. "Just for fun. Just for kicks. Maybe you thought you could just go off somewhere and be free—do whatever you wanted to do whenever you wanted."

Derek's mouth dropped open and he stared at me.

"It wasn't my idea," he repeated. "I was just going along with the guys. I want to stay out of jail, Man, but it's rough!"

"You're telling *me* it's rough!" I said. I wondered what kind of a home he came from. Did his father beat him? Had his parents split up? Did his parents ever take time to listen to him when he felt like talking? I knew one thing for sure—the kid was starved for love.

A police car pulled slowly around the corner, its driver eyeing us. Dick put his arm around Derek's shoulder.

"OK if we pray with you, Derek?" he asked.

"Yeah," Derek murmered.

Dick nodded at me to pray.

"Lord Jesus, please help Derek. You've heard him sharing with us, and You know how lonely he is. Please help him. Help him to see that You really love him, even when it seems that others let him down. Lord, I pray that You will show Derek and his buddies that You want to be their Savior. Amen." My heart was really in my prayer.

We looked up. There were tears in the eyes of that roughneck!

"Thanks, Man," Derek said. Those words were the sweetest I had ever heard.

A few days after the street witnessing incident I stopped at a local grocery store to buy a newspaper for Bonnie. It was there that I found my first convert. It wasn't a spectacular beginning, but the Lord went to a lot of trouble to set up our encounter. In fact, it took awhile for me to realize that the Lord was at work, and that I had not made a stupid error in judgment.

I had worked there during the past summer. The manager who had been my boss had recently been transferred to another city, so I said a special hello to the new one, whose name was Cal.

"I was sorry to see Mike leave," I said. "He was a good boss."

"You worked here?" Cal asked.

"I worked part-time during the summer."

"I need somebody for part-time right now," Cal said. "Why don't you come back to work?"

"We could sure use the money," I said, "but I go to school full-time, and I'm driving a school bus twenty hours a week. That doesn't leave me much time for studying."

"Well, think it over," Cal said.

I thought and I prayed, and the next time I was in the store I told Cal I would take the job. However, after a few days of working in the store I realized I had bitten off more than I could chew. I simply couldn't manage school, study, and two jobs.

"Cal, I'm sorry," I said. "I made a mistake in accepting your offer. It just isn't working out."

"That's OK," Cal said. "A couple other fellows were around looking for a job. I won't have any trouble getting a man. But if you can stay for the rest of the week I'll sure appreciate it."

"Sure, I'll finish out the week," I said.

I was really troubled because I felt I had let Cal down. I told Bonnie I didn't know why in the world I had done anything so stupid. However, God was about to show me that what I had done was not a result of my stupidity but was His divine will. He had placed me in that store for a purpose.

That night I worked with a teen-ager named Paul Carter. Paul and I had been scheduled to work together the night before, but Paul had traded with another employee and gone out and got drunk. When I met him I was again reminded of myself, "the old Larry," and as the evening went on I silently prayed for him many times.

About ten o'clock business slowed down and we began to talk. I told him about the street witnessing I had been involved in a few nights before. I expected him to listen with a kind of blank respect, so I was really surprised by his response.

"Hey, Man, that sounds all right!" he said.

"Lord, I think maybe I've got a prospect!" I prayed silently, deciding to press on just to see how interested Paul was. "You should come to church with me sometime, Paul. I think you might like it."

He was putting some brown paper sacks on the shelves underneath the counter in preparation for the morning rush. I was wondering whether he was going to pretend that he hadn't heard me.

He got his head out from under the counter and said, "I think I'd like to go sometime."

Again I was surprised. Paul wasn't the type to be found in church any more than I had been the type at his age.

"You know, Larry," he said, "I even tried to pray once. I prayed that the light in my room would go out, but nothin' happened."

My heart started pounding. At last I realized that the Lord had set up this whole thing. He had been working on Paul, and He had brought me into Paul's life to reap the harvest!

I wondered how far the Lord would lead me to go with Paul right then. "Paul," I said, "God does answer prayer. In fact, He will even answer your prayers. First though, you have to ask Him to save you and forgive you of your sins. God will listen to your prayers then, I promise, but you've got to be saved from your sins."

I wondered if perhaps I had said too much—if I had run ahead of the Lord. Then I saw him starting to tremble. Tears came to his eyes. God was moving in a mighty way!

"Do you want to get saved, Paul?" I asked him. "Do you want to accept Jesus as your Savior?"

"I don't know how."

"But do you want to?"

His lips were trembling now, and he nodded.

"What do I have to do?"

"It's real simple, Paul," I said. "All you have to do is say, 'Jesus, save me.' Just three words, Paul."

I bowed my head and prayed, "Jesus, please save Paul. Amen." It was a very simple prayer.

Silently I stood there, head bowed, waiting for Paul to pray. No customers came in to stop our prayers. God took care of every little detail.

Suddenly Paul poured out his heart to God. "Jesus," he pleaded, "please save me. I'm an awful sinner. Please come into my heart and save me. And Lord," he continued, "please help me to help others. Let me tell others about You."

Paul lifted his head, and I could see his joy. I grabbed his hand and shook it.

"Praise the Lord, Paul!" I shouted. "Just a minute; I want to get my Bible."

I ran to the back of the store and got my Bible out of my jacket pocket. I wanted to share the Word with Paul and get him acquainted with it right away. I quickly turned to the last chapter of Mark and started reading the last five verses. I soon realized that it was not what I had intended to read, but I didn't care, and neither did Paul.

"He that believeth," I read, "and is baptized shall be saved; but he that believeth not shall be damned."

As Paul and I were reading this verse a man came in who was to teach me that I was not to catch every fish that swam near my net. He was a middle-aged man—sweaty, rumpled, smelly and very, very drunk.

"Wha' ya readin'?" he asked. "My fav'rite book?"

"We're reading the Bible," I replied, a little resentful that he had come in during the moment of glory.

He reached out and grabbed the Bible out of my hand. He cocked his head, tried to focus one eye on the page, and when that didn't work he tried to focus the other eye on it. That didn't work either.

"Print's blurred," he said, handing the Bible back to me. "Don't print things the way they used to. Sloppy workma'ship. Nobo'y does good job thesh days. You read it to me."

"He that believeth and is baptized shall be saved; but he that believeth not shall be damned," I read. At the same time I was silently praying, "Lord, is this another one?"

"Who's the damned?" he asked. Now he was trying to focus his eyes on me.

"Who's the damned?" His voice was growing shrill.

God moved, and I could hardly believe what I heard. The drunk wasn't to be my convert after all. It appeared that he was to be Paul's.

"You're the damned!" Paul told him.

I wanted to speak up, but I restrained myself. After all, Paul had just asked the Lord to help him speak for Him.

"You're the damned," Paul continued, "because you haven't accepted Jesus Christ as your Savior."

"Wow!" I thought. Everything was very quiet. The drunk, braced against the counter, just stood there, his mouth hanging open.

"I wanna ask you gen'lemen something," he said, and he began to cry. "Have you gen'lemen ever met a man whosh happy on the outside and miserable on the inside?"

Paul and I glanced at each other. The Lord seemed to be saying, "Paul has done what I wanted him to. Now you take over." I put my arm around the drunk.

"Well, tha's me," he sobbed. "Happy on the outside and miserable on the inside. Ever'body thinks I'm so happy, but I'm so miserable."

"Friend," I said gently, "why don't you come back and see me tomorrow? We'll have a good talk after you get sobered up."

I didn't know whether he heard me or not, but he turned and staggered out of the store. Paul and I prayed together for him. I hoped that he would return, but he didn't. I never saw him again.

I was locking the back door when Paul said, "Larry, there's one thing I didn't tell you."

"Yeah, what's that?" I said.

"About half an hour before you and me prayed and I asked Jesus to save me, a buddy of mine came in here. He had some LSD with him. I told him I'd meet him after work. We were both going to try it. I'm glad you told me about God. I think He must have sent you to me tonight."

"God always knows what He's doing," I said, marveling at His ways.

I was elated because I had finally witnessed to someone and had led him to Christ. But I knew there was more to Christianity than simply winning them. I knew I needed to get Paul into church, where he could have the fellowship of other Christians. So many of the young people were leaving the church and going into lives of almost unbelievable sin. There were so many pressures facing them at school and in many of their social activities that I knew it was important to get Paul grounded in the faith.

Bonnie and I had planned to go hear Wes preach the following Sunday, and we decided it would be a good idea to invite Paul.

The day after Paul's conversion I asked him if he would like to go with us.

"Yeah, but my old man won't let me," he said. "I went out and got drunk night before last and didn't get home until around 3:00 in the morning. He said I couldn't go out for a week."

"He's right for disciplining you. You deserved it, but I think he'll let you go to church."

"You don't know my old man. He won't let me go anywhere except work," Paul said, sounding disgusted. Secretly, I was glad to hear there were parents who were still willing to take authority over their children. Many of the young people Paul's age thought they were too old for that kind of treatment.

"Yes, he will. First we'll ask Jesus, and then we'll talk to your father. But I'm sure he'll let you go."

"You really believe that?" Paul seemed impressed.

"I really believe it," I told him. "We serve a mighty God. If He could open the Red Sea, then He can influence your father to let you go to church."

"This I've got to see," Paul responded.

"Let's pray right now," I suggested. "That's the first step we need to take."

"OK," Paul said eagerly. "I really would like to go."

"Lord Jesus," I prayed, "Paul has asked You to come into his heart and be his Savior. We thank You for already doing that. Now we have something else to ask of You. Paul would like to go to church. You know that his father is keeping him in for a week. But we believe going to Your house is important, so we're asking You right now to speak to his father and let Paul go to church this Sunday. Thank You for already doing it. Amen."

"Amen," Paul added, not quite sounding convinced.

"Let's go see your earthly father now that we've cleared it with your heavenly Father," I said.

"OK," Paul answered. "I want to believe it, but you sure don't know my old man."

We pulled into Paul's driveway. He lived in an older neighborhood on Owosso's east side. There was a light in the living room, but it was very dark outside, and we had to grope in the darkness to find the door handle on the back door. As we went into the kitchen, we could hear the television.

"Wait here a minute," Paul said. "I'll see if my folks are dressed."

Paul had called earlier in the day and received permission for me to bring him home from work. Evidently his father was very exacting when he laid down an order. Paul came back into the kitchen and motioned for me to follow him into the living room. He introduced me to his folks. Mr. Carter was a lean, balding man in his early fifties, and his wife was a plump, very pleasant woman with a warm smile.

"Larry has something he wants to ask you," Paul said.

"I heard what happened to him last night at work," Mr. Carter said. "I could hardly believe it. Paul is a good boy, but he was headed for trouble. We appreciate what you did for him."

I was surprised and pleased that Paul had testified to his parents about being saved. It made me think of Andrew. The first thing Andrew did was go and win his brother Peter to the Lord.

"The reason I'm here," I said, "is to ask your permission to take Paul to church with me Sunday."

"He can go," his father interrupted.

I looked at Paul, who was staring at his father in disbelief.

"You mean it, Dad?"

"Sure, I mean it. You're not going to get in any trouble in church. I'm glad you're going."

Sunday as we walked into the church, Wes greeted Paul with a big smile.

"Praise the Lord! I'm glad you could come!" he said.

Paul responded to the warmness of Wes and, as the service progressed, we could feel the sweet presence of the Holy Spirit. At the end of the service, Wes extended an invitation for people to come forward.

Paul leaned over and whispered to me.

"I want to go forward so everybody will know I'm a Christian."

"Praise the Lord, Brother! Get on up there!" I said, giving him a push.

As Paul approached the altar, I again breathed a silent prayer of thanks to a wonderful Savior. In two weeks I had made 2,999 fewer converts than Peter had made in one day, but for me to win *one* was a miracle.

Chapter

14

Teen Chapel

It was a warm spring day near the end of my junior year at John Wesley, and I was inching the Karmann Ghia through the downtown traffic. I had the window rolled down, and now I yanked off my tie and unbuttoned the top button on my shirt. I was heaving a long sigh of relief when suddenly an old restaurant on the left side of the street caught my attention. I had left most of the traffic at the bridge which separates downtown Owosso from the residential section, so I pulled the car off to the side and stopped.

The old white frame building appeared to be vacant, and it needed both paint and repairs. As I studied it, I wondered why I was interested in it. I had seen it many times before without really noticing it. It was not an appealing structure in any way, so why this strange and sudden attraction?

Slowly I began to understand. God was speaking to me. I had felt a tremendous burden and compassion for the teen-agers of Owosso. I knew there were many more young people like Paul whom the churches were not reaching. Many times I had prayed, "Jesus, use me to reach these kids."

I had never received an answer to my prayer, but now the answer was coming.

"I want you to rent that building for a teen church," the impression came. It was strong and clear, and I knew that it was God speaking.

"Yes, Jesus," I prayed, "but what about the money? How about the time?" Several questions began to rush through my mind.

"Don't worry about those. I'll take care of all the details. You just trust Me."

I drove on home, feeling the presence of God so near. I really couldn't understand everything that was happening, but I knew that God was moving, and that He had something for me to do.

I went home and prayed, seeking further direction from God. After praying, I went to the phone and called a realtor whom I knew.

"Who owns the little white building just south of the bridge on South Washington Street?" I asked. "It's on the east side of the street."

"I don't know. But I'll find out and call you back in a few minutes," Simmons replied.

"See if it's for rent or for sale," I said.

I hung up the phone and sat down at the kitchen table. I prayed as I waited for him to return the call. The minutes seemed to stretch into hours. Outside, I could hear children playing. Just a few days before, I had heard the two little girls next door to us playing church. The older girl had stood up before her little sister and led the singing, and then began to preach. I wondered if the church would still have that same attraction for her when she became a teen-ager.

"God,' I whispered, "I'm willing to do Your will. Please work out all the details."

A few minutes later the phone rang.

"Larry? Simmons here. That building isn't for sale or for rent. It's owned by Harvey Gladman, who also owns the tavern just south of the building."

My heart sank.

"Ok, Thanks, Mr. Simmons," I said slowly. I hung up the phone and prayed. "Lord, I don't understand, I just don't understand. Was all this just my imagination?"

But again I felt the comforting presence of God.

"Just trust Me."

I continued to pray about the matter, and to wonder what would come of it.

Dick Gleason had again asked me to preach at his church. That Sunday night, after the service, a young lady named Katy came up to me and said, "I enjoyed your sermon. I need to talk with you. Could you spare just a moment?"

"Sure," I said, and we sat down on the front pew.

Katy brushed the hair from her eyes as she began to talk. "It's really strange," she said. "The other day Brother Gleason told me about the project you're starting in Owosso. The day after he told me about it a salesman came to my house selling pots and pans. They were just what I wanted, and I made up my mind to buy them. But just as I was going to tell him I would take them, the Lord began to speak to me. He said, 'Katy, you're willing to spend that money for something you want, but I want you to use it for My work. I want you to take the down payment on those pots and pans, and the monthly payments, and give it to Larry for his work with the teen-agers.' So, I'm going to do what the Lord says."

I could hardly contain my joy.

"Thank you, Katy!" I said, trying to keep my dignity.

What I wanted to do was squeeze her and shout, "Whoopee!"

A few days later, the mailman brought twenty-eight dollars from Katy along with a note saying that she was praying for me and for the work with the teen-agers. I decided it was time to act.

"Jesus," I prayed again, "I'm going to call Mr. Gladman now. I feel that You want me to. I pray that You will speak to him before he even gets my call and take care of this for me."

"Hello, Harvey Gladman speaking." His voice was rough. He made me feel that he wanted me to get right to the point.

"Mr. Gladman, my name is Larry Howland. I'm a student at the college, and I was wondering if you would be interested in renting your building down by the bridge."

"No, I'm not. In fact, I have it rented out right now," he barked. Again I wondered if this plan had really come from God or my own imagination.

"How come you're interested in my building?" Mr. Gladman asked.

"I'm studying for the ministry," I explained, "and I want to start a teen-church, a place where the kids can come and hear the Gospel in a relaxed atmosphere. It won't involve Sundays, but I'll open it on nights when the downtown area is open."

There was a long pause.

"Well now, I think I might be able to do you some good," Mr. Gladman said. "Can you afford seventy-five dollars a month rent?"

"Yes, sir," I told him. I had only twenty-eight dollars, but I would trust God to supply the rest.

"All right," he said, "I'll have the fellow out by Monday. He's a relative of mine, and he's only using it for storage anyway."

"Praise the Lord!" I said, "Thank you, Mr. Gladman!" I hung up and for an hour I praised God for working a miracle. The whole thing was falling into place.

By Monday, I had the rest of the seventy-five dollars. I had not asked anyone for money for the project, but I had prayed about it, and different people had given me money.

A friend came from Detroit and helped me to clean up the building. We scrubbed the floor and the tan walls and got the old restaurant refrigerator working. Then we made a sign that read, "Teen Chapel," a name that had come to me while I was praying. We put the sign in the window. It was a bare-looking place, but we opened the doors for business. As kids came in that day, we talked with them and gave them gospel tracts. Only a few came, but several of them promised to return.

When I got home late that night Bonnie was in bed.

"Wake up, Sleepyhead" I said. "This is no time for sleeping."

"Um . . .," was all I got out of her.

"Come on," I said, "you should be all excited!"

"I'll get excited in the morning," she said sleepily.

I kissed her good night, then knelt down to pray and thank Jesus for what he had done.

A few days later I decided to step out on faith again. I wanted to put something in the Teen Chapel for kids to do. After praying about it, I decided that I would try to get a ping-pong table.

"Lord," I prayed. "I am going to go downtown and try to buy a ping-pong table for the Teen Chapel. If You want me to buy one, then please help me find one for forty dollars." I had never priced a ping-pong table, and had no idea what one would cost, but I wanted to make sure the Lord wanted me to buy one. This seemed like the best way to find out.

I drove downtown to one of the department stores and told the clerk in the sporting goods department that I was looking for a ping-pong table.

"I don't think we have any right now," he said, "but let me call the warehouse and find out."

I prayed silently as he picked up the phone and checked.

"You're in luck," he said, hanging up the phone. "We have one left, and it's been marked down to $39.95. I'll show you what it looks like in the catalog."

"I'll take it!" I said.

"Don't you want to see the picture?" he asked.

"I'll take the table, but you can show me the picture anyway, if you like."

He looked at me as though he really had a case on his hands. He thumbed through the catalog and showed me a picture.

"We can deliver it to you Friday of next week," he said.

"I want it right away," I said.

"Sorry, We can't deliver it any sooner than that."

"If I can get a truck, can I pick it up at the warehouse?" I asked.

"Sure," he said. "Don't see why not."

I phoned Russ, another student who was living at the trailer park. Russ owned a truck, and he agreed to help me pick up the ping-pong table.

Russ and I drove to the warehouse, picked up the table, and took it to the Teen Chapel. As we were carrying it through the chapel door, Russ said, "You haven't got any furniture in here. I have an old couch and chair up at the college that you can have if you want them. They're both in good condition. The wife and I had too much furniture to fit into the trailer so we stored them in the laundry room. We don't want them. If you want them, we can go get them right now and bring them down."

"Do I want them!" I cried. "Let's go!" I was astonished at how God was supplying everything we needed.

Even with the busy time at school, I was able to work in the chapel two nights a week. I chose Fridays and Saturdays since these were the nights the downtown stores were open for business. Driving the school bus twenty-hours a week meant that I often had to study in the chapel while waiting for the young people to come in. Sometimes they would come in one at a time, while at other times there might be as many as ten or fifteen.

Kids with nowhere else to go would come in and play ping-pong. I bought several cases of Coke and gave a free bottle to each of them. Slowly more and more came—just for a free Coke and a game of ping-pong. Every hour on the hour I would have them stop for Bible study. Every time we would finish the Bible study I would ask each kid present if he would like to ask Jesus to come into his heart. Even after two weeks, not one had accepted, but I didn't give up.

I didn't advertise my needs; whenever I needed something I told the Lord about it, and He always provided whatever it was. One of the things I asked for was a record player to use in playing religious records for the kids.

One evening I was visiting with Dick Gleason when Ed, a fellow from Dick's church, stopped by.

"I've been wondering," Ed said, "if you could use an amplifier for your Teen Chapel. I have one that I don't need, and I'd like to give it to you for your work."

"Sure," I said. "I'll find some use for it." I didn't know what on earth I could use an amplifier for.

A week later Ed brought it to the trailer and said, "By the way, it has a record player on it too."

Once again, I praised God for the way He was providing. I explained to Ed that I had been praying for a record player, and that I did not know what I was going to do with the amplifier when he offered it to me.

"Well, I felt I should give it to you," he explained.

That same evening I took the record player down to Teen Chapel and set it up, playing several religious records which had been given to me. I was about to turn the player off and go home when two kids came in. I started to tell them we were closed, but changed my mind. They were dressed in the usual uniform: tattered jeans, dirty tennis shoes and faded blue shirts unbuttoned the whole way down. They weren't wearing undershirts, and I had the impression they thought they looked mighty manly.

"Hi," I said, offering them my hand. "My name's Larry Howland."

Ed and Art introduced themselves briefly, then wandered about the room, inspecting it. I wondered if they had come to ridicule. I went back to the refrigerator and got them each a Coke. When I returned, Ed was setting up the chess set I had brought from home.

"Hey, Man, you play chess?" he said.

"Sure," I said. "Would you like to play a game?"

"Yeah," he responded.

We sat down to play. I was a fair chess player, but it didn't take me long to find out that he was a lot better at chess than I was. He was slowly getting the advantage of me, and I was afraid that if he beat me he would not have much respect for me. I felt that I had to win that game in order to witness to him and to be able to reach him.

"Lord," I prayed silently, "you know how much I would like to see these boys be saved. Please help me

141

beat Ed so they will have more respect for me. Amen."

I sat studying the board. Art was drinking his Coke and watching our moves intently. A couple of moves later Ed made a bad move, and I captured his queen.

"Thank you, Lord," I breathed.

Ed had a puzzled look on his face.

"Man," he said, "I don't make mistakes like that."

"Well, you can't win them all," I told him as I put him in checkmate.

We left the gaming table and sat down on the donated furniture. I began to talk to them about God. Both boys were very open and frank. I turned to Luke and read to them about the woman who had had the issue of blood for twelve years. I explained to them that we were all ill spiritually just as this woman was physically, and that all we had to do was reach out and touch Jesus in prayer in order to be made whole.

Ed was very intelligent and asked many questions.

While we were talking, two girls about thirteen years old walked in. I kept on talking with the boys, and the girls started fooling around with the chess set. They were quiet and kept glancing our way. I wondered if they were listening to our conversation or whether they were just interested in the boys.

Finally I knew it was time.

"Would you fellows like to accept Jesus as your Savior?" I asked. Ed shook his head.

"A little later, Man, a little later," he said.

I looked at Art. He had lit a cigarette and was blowing smoke at the floor. His answer was very soft.

"Yeah," he said, "yeah, I want to."

"All right. I'm going to pray . . . ." I was suddenly interrupted by weeping. I turned and looked at the two little girls. One of them was crying.

"What's your name?" I asked softly.

"Robin," she wept.

"Robin, I asked gently, "would you like to accept Jesus too?"

"Yes," she said.

"All it takes," I told Art and Robin, "are three words, and I want you to pray those three words. Ok?"

They both nodded their assent. I prayed first: "Jesus, please save these kids. They want to take You as their Savior. Please forgive them their sins and help them to be Christians. Amen."

"Now, here are the three words. All you kids have to pray is 'Jesus, save me.'"

Art prayed softly, "Jesus, save me."

We waited as Robin tried to get the words out. She finally managed, "Jesus, save me too. Amen."

I praised God for the way He was moving. Robin told me that she had never been in a church before. That night she had come to Owosso to visit her cousin, and the Lord led them into the Teen Chapel. Even though Robin had not been exposed to the preaching of the Gospel, the Holy Spirit had been working in her life.

As the months passed, several more teen-agers were saved in the Teen Chapel. Many others received much-needed help. It was exciting to see the Lord move. The chapel remained open until August, when another group opened in town with the same basic purpose. As suddenly as God had told me to open the Chapel, He now told me it was time to close. I obeyed.

Chapter
15

John

In November of my senior year I was invited to preach a trial sermon at a Wesleyan church in Flint. The pastor had resigned unexpectedly, and because of the shortage of pastors, the church decided to try a student pastor, willing to use a man who had not yet been ordained.

After I had preached there on two Sundays, Bonnie and I were almost certain that the people would call me as their student pastor. Expecting our future weekends to be all tied up, we decided to visit Bonnie's parents one Friday. They lived in Detroit, so we left Owosso and drove toward Flint, intending to take the expressway to Detroit.

It was snowing heavily, and the temperature was on the low side of zero. As we approached Flint, snowflakes were covering the windshield almost as fast as the wipers cleared them away. Bonnie was coughing from a stubborn cold she had been fighting for days, and I was wishing that we had stayed at home.

"Honey, would you please stop at a drugstore in Flint and get me some cough drops?" she asked—the question broken into short pieces by fits of coughing.

"Sure," I said. "Why don't we stop at that little drug-store that's just down the street from the church? That way we can get the house number of the parsonage and give it to your folks."

"Fine," she wheezed. "Only don't let yourself get too built up about getting that church."

As I drove along, trying to keep control of the car, I had second thoughts about going six miles out of my way just to get an address. Surely there were drugstores closer by. But as I approached the exit that would take us to the church, I felt the Holy Spirit urging me to take it.

"Now what?" I wondered although I was getting to the point in my life where I quit questioning such directions.

The snow began to fall even heavier from a dark sky as we turned down the street where the parsonage and drugstore were both located. The house sat about thirty feet from the road. It looked lonely, as if it could hardly wait for someone to move in. I drove past the house and pulled in at the drugstore.

"What kind of cough drops do you want?" I asked as I started to get out of the car.

Suddenly I stopped. *Walking out of the drugstore and getting into a car was John Morton, Tom's brother!* I could hardly believe my eyes. I was so surprised at seeing John that I didn't say anything. He drove away before I could even think clearly. I got out of the car, walked into the drugstore and bought the cough drops. Then when I came out, I told Bonnie whom I had seen. We knew then that God had brought us to the drugstore so I could see John.

I started the car, and we headed once again for the expressway. It was quiet in the snow-shrouded car, only the sound of the windshield wipers breaking the silence. I thought back to just a few years ago, before John had introduced me to Tom, and we had embarked on the crime spree that had ended in his death.

As we went down the ramp onto the expressway, I remembered our army days and one of the many times that John and I had gone "out on the town" in Fontainebleau. John had started a barroom brawl simply for the fun and excitement of it. He had been one of the toughest guys in the outfit always conscious of his muscles, always proud that he had been a Golden Gloves boxer.

The bright lights of an oncoming car brought my thoughts back to the present. Bonnie was asleep beside me, her cough now quieted. I reached over and turned the radio on and found a station playing soft music. As we neared Detroit, I began to pray for John. "Lord, please help me reach him for You. I know You love him."

As I pulled into my in-laws' driveway, I realized I had forgotten to get the address of the parsonage.

During the few days after our return from Detroit, there was still no word from the church concerning their decision. Bonnie and I waited anxiously, hoping that a decision would soon be made. On Wednesday evening we received a call from the District Superintendent informing us that the church had voted to call me as its pastor.

The following Monday we moved into the house, and I looked up John's name and address in the phone book. He lived only three miles from the church. Now that I had his address and phone number, I didn't know just what to do. I wondered how John would react to me. Would he blame me for his brother's death?

I prayed for him once again as I dialed his number. His wife answered the phone. She squealed when I told her who was calling.

"Larry Howland!" she said. "It's really you? Where on

146

earth are you?"

"I'm living in Flint now, about three miles from you." I explained that I was now a lay minister, and told her where the church was located. She said John had gone to the store, but she would have him call me when he got back.

It wasn't long before the phone rang.

"Larry," John said, his voice booming over the phone, "Clara said you're here in Flint."

"Yes," I replied, "I've been here about a week."

"She also said you're a preacher. She's putting me on, isn't she?" The tone of his voice expressed his doubt.

"Nope. She's absolutely right," I told him.

"I've got to hear about this!" he said. "I'll be right over. How do I get there?"

I told him how to reach the parsonage, and after we had hung up I put on my coat.

"Bonnie, I'm going outside to watch for John," I said. I switched on the front light and walked outside. It was snowing again, and the flakes coming down around the streetlight looked like an army of white moths. As I paced up and down the sidewalk old memories began to torment me. John and Tom. Old times should be remembered as good times, but these memories were not good at all: memories of barroom brawls; memories of pulling a gun and announcing a hold-up; memories of frightened faces with large, round eyes; memories of running, running and more running; memories of dreams that were so terrifying that I would wake up shaking and drenched with perspiration.

As I paced, I began to pray. "Lord Jesus, please help me talk to John. He needs to have You in his life."

Several cars passed our street. We were just off a main road, and I kept expecting each car to be John's. Finally, an older model Pontiac turned slowly down our street and then into our driveway.

John pulled up by the house and got out of the car. I paused, not knowing just what to say or do. John and I had been best friends, but time and circumstances change things. John looked at me, and a big grin came over his face.

"It sure is good to see you, Larry."

"Same here," I said. We shook hands and then embraced. I was glad to see him even if he did remind me of the past.

"Come on in," I said. "I want you to meet my wife."

We drank hot coffee and talked about the weather, and then John grew earnest, and I had a feeling I knew what he was going to ask me.

"I've always wondered if Tom was killed right away. Or did he suffer?" John asked. He had loved his brother.

"He was killed instantly," I said, the scene still vivid in my mind. "He never knew what hit him."

We sat in silence for a few minutes. I was hearing again the explosive shot that had killed Tom. I was feeling the horror, the fear. But something else was troubling me too.

"I have a question for you, John," I said. I wasn't sure that I really wanted to hear the answer to this one. "Did Tom ever attend church much? What I mean is—did he know about God?"

"Sure he did," John said. "We used to attend a little Pentecostal church when we were kids."

I hated to hear those words. I had tried to hold onto the hope that somehow Tom had never heard the Gospel, and that God's judgment of him would have been less severe than one who had heard the Gospel and rejected it. But I believe that all the time I had known better. I realized that he knew the difference between right and wrong.

The only hope I could hold onto now was that Tom had received his judgment from a just and loving God. I tried not to think about it any longer, but determined to be more diligent in bringing the message of Christ to those who were in the same shape that Tom and I had once been in.

John and I talked until after midnight, and then he left for home. Before he left, he confided in me that his drinking problem had become very severe. Although neither one of us voiced it, it was clear that John could well be classified as an alcoholic. That night as I went to bed, I asked God once again to give me the opportunity to see John saved. I felt the words of the chorus in my heart, "And may I humbly do my part to win that soul for Thee."

I saw John quite often after that. Two weeks later he and Clara and the children came to church. Every time I talked with John, I told him that Jesus loved him and wanted him to commit his life to Him.

"Keep praying for me, Larry," he told me one day. "Just don't give up."

"You don't have to worry about that," I assured him. "I'm not going to give up on you."

One evening while Bonnie and I were eating supper John phoned.

"Clara wants to see you right away," he said. "She says she wants to become a Christian. She's waiting at the house, and I told her I would call you."

"How about you?" I asked.

"Not yet, Larry. I'm at a bar right now. I need some more time to think about all of this."

I hung up, and Bonnie and I hurried to John's house. I asked Clara if she understood what she wanted to do.

She nodded yes, and tears began to roll down her cheeks.

149

"Pray and ask God to forgive you of your sins," I instructed her. "And then ask Jesus Christ to be your Savior. It's that simple."

We knelt down, and I prayed that Clara would have the faith to believe that Jesus could save her right now.

"Now you pray," I encouraged her.

She struggled for words, and then she prayed, "Please, dear Jesus, please save me. I want to be a Christian. I'm sorry for all of my sins. And please save John, too. Amen."

It was such a simple prayer, but the Lord loves simple prayers. Bonnie and I went home after telling Clara to continue, along with us, to pray for John.

Two days later I was reading my Bible and praying for John when he came to the door. I knew the Lord had sent him by.

"I want to know something, John," I said as he sat down on the couch. "Were you ever in that drugstore before the night I saw you there?"

"No," he admitted.

"Do you realize we came six miles out of our way just to buy cough drops for Bonnie? I almost didn't come, but I felt the Lord telling me to come."

John looked up, surprised. I had told him that I had seen him coming out of the drugstore that night, but I had never explained the circumstances. His hands began to shake as he took a cigarette out of his pocket. He tapped the end of the cigarette on his lighter.

"Clara wasn't feeling well that day," he explained, "and she asked me to go get her some Alka Seltzer. I was just driving around and happened to see that drugstore." He smiled a crooked little smile. "Say, that's really a coincidence, isn't it?"

I chuckled, thinking how perfect God's timing is.

"There are no coincidences with God, John. He caused

our paths to cross that night because He loves you. He wants you to give your life to Him."

John got up and walked out into the kitchen and I followed him.

"I just don't know," he said impatiently. "I don't know if I'm ready yet."

"Do you think Jesus dilly-dallied when the Roman soldiers told Him to spread His arms out on the cross?" I asked.

John walked back into the living room, with me at his heels.

"He did that for you," I continued, "because He loves you."

John walked to the kitchen again.

"I think I'm going home," he muttered, heading toward the back door.

"You can't, John," I replied. "The door is right there, but you know you can't walk through it. Try it. You can't do it." I was praying silently, "Oh, Jesus, please don't let John get away."

John was staring at me. I knew his temper, and for a moment I was afraid of him. I knew what he could do if he felt that I had pushed him too far.

"You're right," he said. "I can't." He walked back into the living room and sat down on the sofa. Suddenly his mild trembling became a violent shaking, and he dropped to his knees, crying like a child.

"Oh, God," he cried, "please help me! Please, *save me!*"

Kneeling, I began to pray with him. What a beautiful sight it was to see John broken by the Lord! What a thrill to see that 245-pound boxer suddenly become a child of God!

It was still pitch dark when the phone rang early the

next morning. Sleepily I crawled out of bed and went to answer it.

"Praise the Lord!" I recognized the wide-awake, cheerful voice. It was John, and he sounded jubilant.

"Praise the Lord!" I said, trying to stifle a yawn.

"Praise the Lord, Brother!"

"Praise the Lord," I said again. I think I had one eye open by now. "I'm glad you're feeling this way, John, but I'm wondering whether you had something else to say to me maybe."

"Yeah," he said, "I want to go out tonight and tell some of my old buddies what's happened. I want to witness to them, and I want you to go with me!"

I told him I'd go along, and then after hanging up the phone I went and sat on the edge of the bed for a long time, just marveling. The Holy Spirit had done it again! An old hymn came to me, and in my mind I was singing, "What a Friend We Have in Jesus." Anyone who can take a criminal like myself and an alcoholic like John and transform them into Sons of the Living God is a Friend indeed.

Chapter
16

"I Was In Prison and Ye Came Unto Me"

It was graduation day. I felt awkward in the long, flowing academic gown, and my neck was stiff from holding my head steady so my mortar board wouldn't fall off, but I was awfully happy. The afternoon sun was warm, the air was sweet, and the only sound was the shuffling of our feet as "my class" marched out of the Administration Building and down the long, winding walk to the gymnasium where the baccalaureate address would be given. My heart was singing. I had made it! By the grace of God I had made it through college, and I was graduating with honors. Praise God! I was wishing that my old high school teachers could see me now; it would boggle their minds.

We paraded into the gym, and the waiting crowd turned to watch us. They looked so proud, so happy as they stood on tip-toe, stretching their necks in an effort to catch a glimpse of their own graduates. I caught a glimpse of Bonnie, and just then she saw me; she smiled and I winked.

We took our seats in front of the podium, and the service began. It is blurred in my mind, for I kept thinking about the old days. How far away they seemed. Even four

153

years before, a college degree would hardly have seemed possible—yet here I sat, waiting to receive my diploma.

After several more preliminaries, the academic dean began calling the names of the graduates and awarding the diplomas.

"Larry Howland," the dean said directly into the microphone.

Bonnie snapped a picture as I received my "sheepskin." All I could think was, "Thank You, Lord Jesus. I know this comes from You."

After the formalities, Bonnie and I hurried home to Flint for the reception she had planned. Both her parents and mine had travelled many miles to share this occasion with us.

It was a few days after the graduation service before I could realize that I had really made it. How wonderful God is! Bonnie teased me as I framed my diploma and hung it on the wall of my study.

On the following Tuesday I was brought completely back to the task at hand. Bonnie was shopping, and the coffee had just started to perk when I heard a knock at the door. It was Wes Smith.

"Wes!" I exclaimed, delighted to see him. "Come on into the kitchen and sit down. You're just in time for a cup of coffee."

I got out two mugs and filled them with the steaming brew.

"I had to come to Flint on some business," Wes said, "so I thought I'd drop in. There's something I've been wanting to talk with you about."

"What's on your mind?" I asked. "I think I'm ready for just about anything now."

"Larry, how would you like to go to Jackson Prison and share your testimony?"

"Wow!" I said. "When do we go?"

"In about two weeks," Wes replied. "There's a **Full** Gospel group going in once a month, and they've invited me to go along. I thought maybe you'd like to go too."

Wes knew that for some time it had been my dream to be able to take the Gospel to the men in prison. I knew that there were many people behind bars who were not being reached with the message of Jesus Christ. I thought of them often. How were they ever going to hear the story of salvation? In general they seemed to be a forgotten breed. Jesus' words kept coming to me, "I was in prison, and ye came unto Me."

I realized that I would have to be responsible for the burden God was giving me for these men. And now God was giving me an opportunity to share His Word with many lonely and forsaken men.

Two weeks later when I arrived at Wes's home in St. Johns, he said, "There are complications, Larry. The prison has a rule that forbids former inmates from going back in."

My heart sank.

"However," Wes continued, "we serve a miracle-working God. The warden has given special permission for you to go in and preach."

As we entered the prison with the Full Gospel workers, all of the ugly old memories came flooding back to me. Everything looked the same. It was just as dreary and frightening as it had ever been. The fact that I knew I could come back out was only partially comforting. There was still the same foreboding feeling that this could be a one-way journey. We passed through security, and then into a large rotunda. After this we were ushered into a long hallway leading into the "yard." As we walked through the yard, we passed several prisoners, some in groups and some sitting alone. Just to the left of our route to the chapel two teams of prisoners were engaged in a game of basketball.

Several of the men noticed the Bibles we were carrying. "Hey, Man," one of them said for us to hear, "here come the preachers ready to put a shuck on anybody who'll listen."

"Amen, Brother," one of his friends added.

We kept walking toward the chapel. I could understand the resentment many of the men felt toward religion and the church. To them, it seemed that we offered nothing. All of their lives they had observed materialism, ritualism, and piety without really seeing that Jesus Christ *does* offer deliverance from sin. Many of them had heard preachers *telling* what Jesus Christ could do, but few of them had ever observed a Christian *showing* what Jesus Christ could do to set a person free. My heart went out to them. I knew many of them had never known anything but a life of crime. Reared in families without fathers, with no moral or Christian guidance, they had grown up to rebel against every kind of authority, and especially against a religion that held its hand out to receive rather than to give.

These thoughts were still going through my mind as we moved on to the chapel. Once there, the guard left us and we were on our own.

I looked into the rough faces of the men gathered there, and I loved them. Mentally and emotionally, I was wearing my old uniform, and I knew their sufferings. Their scars were my scars. Their fears had been my fears, their yearnings my own. I could say with awful truth, "There, but for the grace of God, go I." Except for the grace of God, I would be one of them, facing a life sentence without any hope. But, by the grace of God, I was free, and I had returned to tell them how they too could be free —even though they were prisoners.

As I sat there waiting for my turn to speak, I bowed my head and began to pray. "Lord Jesus," I said, "You will have to do it all. I know I can't do anything on my own. I don't know what I should even say to them. Please send Your Holy Spirit to help me. Amen."

My turn came, and I walked to the pulpit, hotly conscious that every eye in the chapel was on me. Suddenly the Lord gave me a thought.

"How many of you fellows are from Flint?" I asked, holding my right hand high in the air. Many other hands went up. "So am I!" I said, and the ice was broken.

"Turn with me to Mark 5:18-19," I said, and there was a scramble for Bibles. "I want to tell you how Jesus healed a demon-possessed man, and how He cast the demons out of the fellow," I said. Then I read the Scripture:

And when he was come into the ship, he that had been possessed with the devil prayed him that he might be with him. Howbeit Jesus suffered him not, but saith unto him, Go home to thy friends, and tell them how great things the Lord hath done for thee, and hath had compassion on thee.

"Jesus told this man to go home to his friends and tell them what great things He had done for them," I said. "Today Jesus has sent me home to you, my friends, and told me to tell you what great things He has done for me."

Suddenly somebody shouted, "Amen!" and someone else said, "Praise the Lord!" I knew I had at least two fellow Christians in that room already. I went on to tell of my former life, and I could see the hard mask dropping from many faces. They accepted me. I told them of what Jesus Christ had done for me—how He had improved my mind, my morals, and every part of my life. When I finished giving my testimony, the men applauded, thanking me with their applause. I knew they were not only thanking us for coming, but they were also thanking us for caring.

An invitation was given, and about seven men came forward. We prayed with each of them.

"I don't know if God will forgive me," one giant black told Dick, one of the Full Gospel workers.

"God will forgive you," Dick assured him.

"But I killed a man, and I'm serving a life sentence."

"God will still forgive you," Dick persisted.

"But," the convict said, "I did it for fun."

It was this type of man whom God was reaching.

There were no guards in the chapel. All of us were somewhat apprehensive. But we knew that we were in the hands of God, and He would do or let be done to us only what He wanted.

After we had prayed with the men at the altar, another inmate came up to Wes and me. "Do you remember me, Larry?"

He was a fellow about my age with enormous arms. He looked as if he could tear a telephone book in two.

"No, not off hand," I replied. I was wishing I could recall him.

"I was with you in quarantine when you first came into Jackson. My name's Skip Brock."

I did not remember Skip, but after we talked awhile, we were like old friends. He was a member of the Outlaws, a motorcycle gang, and was in prison on an armed-robbery charge. He had only eight days to go, and then he faced another year in a federal institution on a different charge. As we talked, I could sense the Holy Spirit was dealing with him.

"Would you like to give your heart to Jesus?" Wes

asked him.

He nodded, and tears began to roll down his cheeks. We asked him to kneel at the altar and ask Jesus to forgive him of his sins.

Skip knelt, and as sincerely as anyone in any church ever has, he asked Jesus to become his Savior.

I walked out of the prison that day rejoicing and thanking God. He had manifested Himself in a wonderful way. I thought of Jesus' words in Luke 4:18: "The Spirit of the Lord is upon me, because he hath annointed me to preach the gospel to the poor; he hath sent me to heal the brokenhearted, to preach deliverance to the captives, and recovering of sight to the blind, to set at liberty them that are bruised."

I knew I could express the sentiments of most of the men in the chapel that day: "Thank You, Lord Jesus, for caring. Thank You for setting us free!"

Chapter
17

Your Adversary the Devil

Our monthly trips to the prison continued, and I was amazed at the way God was opening doors for us to reach so many people who had no contact whatever with any church or religious organization. However, there were occasions when the open doors slammed shut in my face, leaving me puzzled and frustrated. One door slammed particularly hard; behind it was a girl named Margie.

Several days before Thanksgiving, just as I was about to leave for a speaking engagement, the phone rang. It was one of the men involved in the prison ministry at Jackson.

"Larry, there's a gal in Flint I'd like you to look up," he said. "Name's Margie Evans. She read one of Nicky Cruz's tracts and then wrote to the address on the back and said she was going to commit suicide. They called me to see if I knew someone in Flint who could help her."

"Where does she live?" I asked.

He gave me the address, and I said, "I'll go see her as soon as I can!" Looking at my watch, I made a quick calculation. No, it was impossible; I couldn't break my engagement at this late hour. Margie would have to wait until the following day.

The next day I got into my car and headed for her home in a rough part of town. Approaching her address, I had to slow down to keep from hitting boney dogs and ragged kids playing in the street. Yards were littered with trash. Front porches sagged. Some houses had boarded-up windows.

I wondered what I was going to say to Margie. How do you help someone who is so desperate she is ready to commit suicide? I hoped that I was not too late. It must have taken a couple of days for them to get the letter and then to call Don, so it must have been at least three days since she had written her plea for help.

I found her house and pulled up to the curb. "Lord, show me how to help Margie, and what I should say."

A middle-aged black woman opened the door about half way and looked out at me suspiciously.

"What do you want?" she asked.

"Is this the Evans' residence?"

"What about it?"

"I'm looking for Margie Evans. I'm a preacher."

The woman threw back her head and laughed.

"Yeah, that's what Margie needs all right! She needs a preacher!"

"Is she here?" I asked.

"Nope, I ain't seen her for two days."

"Are you Mrs. Evans?" I asked.

"Yeah, I'm Mrs. Evans."

"Look, your daughter may be in trouble." I could see I was not getting through to her, and yet I didn't know what else to say. "I believe Margie is very emotionally upset. Do you know where I could possibly find her?"

"Sorry, Mister, but she comes and goes as she pleases."

I could hardly believe I was speaking to the mother of a teen-age daughter who had been missing for two days. I

161

took out a card with my name and phone number on it.

"Would you please have her call me if she comes home? It is very important."

Mrs. Evans took the card and closed the door. I had no idea if she would relay my message or not.

Bonnie was working in the kitchen when I arrived home. I told her about the response of Mrs. Evans. We agreed to pray for Margie and ask the Lord to somehow impress it upon her not to do anything foolish until someone could get to her with the Gospel message. My heart cried out for all the young people who were living such lives, and living in homes where parents obviously did not care whether their children lived or died.

For the next two days I kept waiting for the phone to ring. Every time it did ring, I prayed it would be Margie. Finally I decided to call her and see if I could find her at home. Her mother answered the phone on the second ring.

"May I speak with Margie, please?" I thought it better not to identify myself.

"She's not here." She hung up the phone.

Still not able to make contact with Margie, we left for Dayton, Ohio the day before Thanksgiving to visit Mom and my stepfather and my adopted stepsister. We had a pleasant visit but could only stay two days. It was on the return trip that I was to learn what the Psalmist had meant when he wrote, "For he shall give his angels charge over thee, to keep thee in all thy ways."

As we returned home from vacation Bonnie drove and I attempted to study. I was finding it difficult to read under those conditions and finally, I gave up.

"If you'll take the next exit, I'll drive the rest of the way. I can't seem to study and ride at the same time," I said.

"Good. I'm getting tired anyway," Bonnie said. She

pulled off at the next exit, and I took over the wheel. We had been back on the expressway for less than a minute when Bonnie noticed something farther down the road.

"What's that smoke?" she asked.

My heart seemed to stop. The "smoke" was a dust cloud whirling toward us at fantastic speed. I leaned closer to the windshield. A vehicle! A car on the wrong side of the road! And four more cars hurtling after it! I hit the brake.

"Dear God!" I prayed.

I could see them clearly now. Four police cars chasing another car—all coming about a hundred miles an hour. The police cars were crossing the median strip. Now all five were bearing down on us. Frantically I twisted the steering wheel, trying to maneuver out of their path. Which way to go? Would they stay in formation? Or would they split? The lead car was off the road now. Down into the ditch. Up again! It was heading toward us. Now it was on the berm, its side snapping off the posts of the guardrail. Thump. Thump. Thump. They sounded like giant match sticks. Through the guardrail! Over the embankment! Out into the field.

It stopped at last. Everything seemed to stop. Then a man leaped from the first car and began running across the field and patrolmen seemed to pour from the other cars. One had a gun in his hands.

"He's going to shoot!" Bonnie screamed, covering her ears with her hands and burying her face in my shoulder.

"No," I said. "It's OK. The guy surrendered. He's just standing there with his hands in the air."

I headed down the expressway again, and Bonnie wiped the tears from her eyes.

"That was close!" she shuddered.

"Thank You, Lord, for keeping us from harm," I prayed.

163

It was just now dawning on me that we had come close to being killed.

"Oh, I'm so glad we changed seats," Bonnie said. She was still shaking, still dabbing at her eyes and blowing her nose. "I don't know what I would have done!" My generally imperturbable little wife was now giggling almost hysterically. "Oh, isn't it wonderful how the Lord does look after us!"

Bonnie moved closer to me.

"Wouldn't Satan have cheered if he could have gotten rid of us!" she said.

From that time on, Bonnie and I both were keenly aware of our reliance upon God. We knew He was taking care of us.

When we arrived home I thought about Margie and wondered what to do. I was sure I would not receive a welcome if I returned to her house. I decided that the best course of action would be to call and hope that she answered the phone.

I dialed the number and listened for the ring.

"Lord, please don't let anyone else answer that phone," I prayed.

"Hello?"

"Margie?"

"Yes, who is this?" Her voice was very soft and low so that I could hardly hear.

"Margie, this is Larry Howland. I'm a minister, and after you wrote to the address on that tract you read, they called me and asked me to get in touch with you."

"I don't need any help," she said. "That's been over a week since I wrote that letter. I could be dead by now."

"Didn't your mother tell you I had been there to see you a week ago Friday?"

"My old lady don't tell me nothing but 'Shut up' and

164

'Get out of the house!' ''

"I would like to meet with you."

"No!" she said, for the first time raising her voice.

"Would you like to talk about your problem on the phone?"

"No, and if you don't shut up, I'm going to hang up."

"No, wait a minute! Don't hang up!'' The phone slammed down. I sat at my desk feeling frustrated and helpless.

I shared my thoughts with Bonnie and we again made Margie a matter of prayer. We did not know what else to do.

The next day when I came home for lunch Bonnie was obviously excited about something.

"Margie called, and she wants you to call her back. But she's not home. She gave me a number for you to call."

I went straight to the phone and dialed the number.

"Margie, this is Larry Howland again. I'm glad you called and wanted to talk to me."

There was nothing but silence. For a moment, I thought she had hung up again. Then I could hear her crying softly.

"Margie, what is it? Tell me what's wrong? I want to help."

"Nobody cares," she said softly, still crying. "I'm hooked on drugs, I just had an abortion, everything is a mess, but nobody cares. Please help me, *please*."

"Where are you? I'll come right now."

"No, you can't come here. I'll come to your church."

Margie assured me she could get transportation to the church. We decided we would meet at seven o'clock in my study. I went early and prayed for Margie, waiting expectantly for her to arrive. I looked at the clock. It was ten minutes past seven. I thought about the things we had learned in the classroom. I appreciated John Wesley College, and I appreciated my professors. They were dedicated men and women. Every one of them had a Christian testimony. Many of them had been pastors and missionaries before joining the faculty at the college. But, for all of their learning, they had not prepared me for anything like this. Soon it was seven-thirty, and then eight o'clock. I finally gave up and went home and once again shared my frustrations with Bonnie.

Over the next few days, Margie called several times. She told me never to call her at her home, so I respected her wish and always waited for her to call me.

During one of her calls, as she poured out her heart to me, I suggested we pray. "If you pray, I'll hang up!" she told me.

"But, Margie, God is the only one who can really help you. He is the one person you can count on."

Margie hung up.

The last time we had contact with Margie, she called and Bonnie answered the phone. Bonnie tried to talk to her about her only hope, Jesus Christ. Margie listened without saying a word.

"Are you still there?" Bonnie asked her.

"Yes, but I might as well be dead. Nobody can help me," she said, hanging up for the last time.

I had never met anyone like Margie. Even in prison, men seemed to have more hope than Margie. Men on death row looked hopefully to the day they would have their sentence commuted to life imprisonment. But Margie was different. She felt forsaken and lonely, and even incapable of responding to our many offers of assistance. I wish I could tell her we still care.

166

Chapter

18

Ex-Con and Ex-Cop Go to Jail

My experience with Margie had left me somewhat shaken. But I knew that there were many others who needed help, and I still had a ministry to carry out. I was soon to learn that God was going to open up another area of outreach.

One Thursday evening I attended a revival service where Wes was speaking. Immediately after the closing prayer, he motioned for me to come up to the front. Standing by him was a large, muscular fellow I had never met before.

"Larry," Wes said, "I want you to meet a friend of mine, Doug Hall."

Doug smiled as he reached out to shake hands with me.

"Praise the Lord, Brother! It's really good to meet you," he said. "I've sure heard a lot about you."

I guessed Doug to be about forty years old. I had heard that he had been a Marine drill instructor and a city policeman in Flint, with a reputation for being a mean instructor and a tough cop. He had a look on his face that made you know that here was a man who could set his mind to something and stick by it.

The following Monday, Doug called me and asked me to come over to his house, saying he had something he wanted to talk over with me.

He lived in a nice home just outside the city limits of Flint. He greeted me enthusiastically at the door.

"Praise the Lord, Brother! It sure is good to see you again."

I sat down and Doug served me a cup of coffee, as I waited expectantly to see what he had to talk to me about. Somehow, I could sense that the Holy Spirit was at work in this meeting.

Doug looked at me very seriously.

"Larry," he asked, "how would you like to go into the county jail here in Flint as the chaplain and work with the inmates?"

My heart flipped. I recalled my own pitiful gropings toward the Lord when I was in San Quentin, lonely, frightened, and heartsick. My heart went out to other hungry men behind the prison bars. I wanted to run to them—not tomorrow or next week, but now—and say, "Hey, guys, I've got Good News!" But there was a hitch.

"You know as well as I do that neither one of us would meet the Council of Churches standards for chaplains," I said. I had heard that most prison chaplains were required to have seminary training. "I'm not even ordained."

"Yeah, Brother, but God can open the door," Doug said with real conviction.

I agreed with him that God could open the doors for us.

Doug went on, "I'm going to write a letter to Jonathan Sands, the chairman of the Board of County Commissioners and see what he thinks. I'll tell him about your record, and how you've been wanting to work with prisoners. How's that sound?"

"Beautiful," I replied.

"Then let's pray right now that God will speak to them before they even get my letter."

Doug and I knelt down by the kitchen table. It grew very quiet as I began to pray. "Lord Jesus, You have heard our conversation, and we believe that the things we have been talking about are things You would like to see accomplished. So right now we thank You for what You are going to do. We thank You that we are going to be able to go into the jails in this city and witness to the men there. Amen."

"Amen," Doug agreed.

Four days later Doug called again.

"We've got an appointment with the chairman of the Board of County Commissioners and the head of the Probation Department here in Flint."

"You mean he's answered your letter already?" I asked.

"Better than that," Doug said. "He called instead of writing. He wants us to come this Tuesday. Think you can make it?"

Doug picked me up on Tuesday, and we drove to the County Building. It was another beautiful day, and the sunshine seemed to be a symbol of God's approval shining down from heaven.

As we rode the elevator up to Mr. Sands' office, we prayed again. "Lord, please speak to the hearts of these men right now. We believe You won't let them say anything but yes."

We were ushered into Mr. Sands' office by his secretary. Mr. Sands rose from a chair behind his huge desk with his hand extended.

"Gentlemen," he said, "I've been waiting to meet you. You must be Larry Howland," he said to me.

We shook hands, and I took an immediate liking to this

man. Mr. Leonard, the head of the Probation Department, arrived soon after we did. He was a short, plump man with a winning smile. After the introductions, we were all seated and Mr. Sands said, "Go right ahead, gentlemen. Tell us just what you have in mind."

Doug and I looked at each other. He nodded for me to speak first. I knew by the look on his face that he would be praying for me as I spoke. I hesitated, breathed a short silent prayer, and then began.

"Both of you men know about my background," I said, "and I want to get straight to the point. The only reason I'm sitting here in your office today is because of what Jesus Christ has done for me. I was convicted in California of auto theft, and here in Michigan of armed robbery. As you know, I served time in both states. And in spite of all the efforts being made by the authorities to rehabilitate men, I don't believe the system did one thing to help me. It was God who changed my life in the county jail.

"I believe this is where we need to reach the men," I continued. "Here in the county jail you have men who are still on this side of prison. I feel that we can help these fellows if you will give us the chance. Rather, *Jesus Christ* can help them. I feel very strongly that if God can get to them now, we will save men from prison later. I guarantee you that you will see lives changed."

I continued pouring my heart out as Doug prayed for the Holy Spirit to speak to them. Finally I finished, and the room was silent.

Mr. Leonard was the first to speak. "Well," he said, "we certainly can't argue with success, can we? After all, you are evidence of the success you're arguing for. As far as I'm concerned, you have my OK to implement the program."

I looked at Mr. Sands as Mr. Leonard said, "How about

170

you, John? What do you think?"

Mr. Sands had a very strange look on his face. I hadn't noticed until then that the Holy Spirit had been dealing with him as I spoke. He fought to keep the tears back.

"Yes," he said, "I'm for it, very definitely."

"Good!" Mr. Leonard said. "That leaves only one obstacle."

"What obstacle now?" I wondered. I thought this was all the clearance we needed. Mr. Leonard shifted in his chair. "We will have to get the clearance of the sheriff. He has the final authority over anything going on in his jail."

I knew that this would be no obstacle, as I could sense the Holy Spirit at work, putting every piece together perfectly.

A few days later Mr. Leonard called.

"Mr. Howland," he asked, "would you possibly be able to meet with the sheriff, Mr. Hall, and me next Tuesday at 9:30 A.M.?"

"Sure," I said, without even checking the calendar. I knew nothing could be more important than this.

The days passed slowly. Each day I prayed and asked God to touch the sheriff's heart before we even got to his office. Doug and I were both given the assurance that God was opening the door.

Tuesday at 9:30, the three of us were shown into the sheriff's office. He was a tall, distinguished-looking man with a firm handshake.

"Would you like a cup of coffee, gentlemen?" he asked. I was surprised that a man of his importance would waste time drinking coffee with an ex-convict.

As we sat down to drink our coffee, the sheriff looked at Mr. Leonard.

"Well, let's have it."

"Go ahead, Larry," Mr. Leonard said, nodding at me.

171

I said much the same thing that I had said in Mr. Sands' office. I could see Doug praying as I spoke. As soon as I finished talking, Doug took it up. He told how he felt that he and I could reach some of the fellows in the jail, and possibly keep them from a prison sentence later on.

"Keep talking, Doug," I thought. He was doing a better job than most attorneys could do.

"Ok, fellows," the sheriff suddenly interjected. "You've sold me. You can start on the second floor next Friday."

"Thank you, Sheriff," I said. "We appreciate this opportunity very much." I sounded so dignified as I spoke, but inside I was shouting, "Whoopee! Praise the Lord!" As we left the building it was all I could do to keep from dancing.

On Friday, Doug and I were ushered into the elevator and taken to the second floor of the county jail. The officer walked with us to the tank and unlocked the door. The tank is the area at the end of the tier where the men are allowed to congregate. The sheriff had made the decision to start us on the second floor as these were men confined on lesser charges, and were less of a security risk.

"I'm going to lock you in," he said. "I'll be back up in about half an hour to let you out."

We walked into the tank, not really knowing what to expect. Most of the guys were sitting around playing cards or reading books. Men such as these who were not serious security risks were not forced to spend all their time in their cells. They looked up at us curiously, wondering what was up. I quickly decided the only thing to do was to begin by addressing the entire group.

"Fellows," I began, "we would like to talk with you for a minute. If you don't want to listen, then you're free to go back to your cells. You don't have to give us your time, but we are here to help you."

I continued, telling them our names and our backgrounds.

"I spent a year and a half in San Quentin, and did some small time in Jackson. Doug and I are here to help you."

It grew quiet, just as it had in Mr. Sands' office. No one was moving now. All the cards had been put aside, and all the books were closed. I could sense the power of the Holy Spirit.

"Fellows," I said, "we've come to bring you Good News! We're here with you because God loves you and we love you! Jesus Christ sent us to tell you that He died for you. And we want to help you in any way we can. If we can pray with you, visit your families, or counsel with you, we'll be glad to do it. However, we were instructed not to get involved in your cases. Feel free to stay here and talk with us, or whatever you want to do. We're going to be here for awhile. If you want to talk with us, we'll be glad to talk with you."

A few of the guys went back to their cells, and Doug and I talked to some of the others. Several of the men came up to us and started pouring out their troubles. One prisoner was an alcoholic who just couldn't seem to get his life straightened out.

"I'd sure like to pray with you, Danny, if it's all right."

"Yeah, sure, Man. Go ahead."

We sat down and Danny bowed his head. I offered a simple prayer that God would help him to overcome his problem and help him get out of jail. As I said "Amen" and looked up, Danny had tears in his eyes, probably the first he had shed since he was a child. I never cease to marvel at how the Holy Spirit can wring tears out of hearts of stone, but He does it over and over again. And I've noticed that it's the hardest rocks that seem to have the

173

most water in them!

He shook my hand and squeezed hard to show his gratitude.

"Please come back, will ya?" He sounded almost desperate.

"We'll be back next week," I promised.

Doug was talking with a fellow at the other end of the tank. He heard the guard coming, said a short prayer, and we left to meet the guard at the door.

"How'd it go?" the guard inquired.

"Terrific!" I said.

Chapter
19

A Death and a New Birth

Life was exciting. Every morning I wakened up wondering what surprise the Lord had in store for me. Sometimes the calendar in my study was so full of notes I could hardly read the dates: "Monday—visit prison"; "Tuesday —speak at Kalamazoo"; "Wednesday—speak at Shelby."

After the Kalamazoo talk Bonnie and I drove to Shelby to spend the night with Dick and Beverly Workman. Dick is a minister and an old friend.

"Would you like to make some calls with me, Larry?" Dick said at the breakfast table Wednesday morning.

"Sure," I said. "I'll be glad to go along." I was wondering what the Lord had planned for us.

We drove a short distance out of town to a farm owned by a family named Page. Dick had met Mr. Page on one of his hospital visits.

Knocking on the front door, we heard Mr. Page shouting from indoors, "Come around to the back!"

As we approached the back door, Mr. Page poked his head out and said, "Hi, Pastor! We don't use the front door." He was a man about fifty years old with a friendly smile.

"I want you to meet a friend of mine," Dick told him, turning to me. "This is Larry Howland, a fellow who spent some time in prison before he was converted. He's going to speak for us tonight."

We exchanged greetings, and then went into the kitchen and met Mrs. Page. They invited us to sit down, and Dick did not waste any time before he began talking to them about their need to receive Jesus Christ.

"I sure wish you would give your hearts to the Lord," Dick told them.

"Yes, I know we should," Mr. Page replied.

His wife nodded her agreement. "Let us think about it, Reverend. I'd like for you to talk with us about it again."

Mr. Page turned to me. "You've spent some time in prison?"

"Yes," I replied. "I was in San Quentin before I was saved."

"Well, there's a fellow in the county jail I really feel sorry for. Maybe you could help him."

"Who is he?" I asked.

"Name's Craig Hanley," Mr. Page said, pausing to roll a wad of tobacco from one jaw to the other. "Right now he's in the Muskegon County Jail, but I don't figure he'll be there much longer."

"You mean he's getting out?" Dick asked.

"Nope. 'Fraid not. This fellow has a big problem. He's in for murder. Fact is he killed his own son. Baby boy only fifteen months old."

My blood chilled. I had known some tough customers, but I had never met a man who had murdered his own baby.

"Why did he do it?" I asked.

"Wife decided to divorce him," Mr. Page explained. "Then they sort of resolved their problems and figured on staying together after all. But things got worse, and one day Craig just couldn't take it. His mind snapped, and he shot that baby right in the head. Then he turned the rifle on hisself. Way I heard it the bullet went up into his mouth, but it hit a tooth and gee-hawed off. Happened several months ago. He's recovered now, and they have him down in the county jail waiting to be sentenced." Mr. Page leaned forward in his rocking chair and spit into a tin can that was sitting on the floor.

"Used to work with me in the gas station," Mr. Page continued. "Couldn't ask for a nicer young fellow. And he really loved that little boy of his. He just couldn't take it, that's all."

Mr. Page walked over to a kitchen cupboard and pulled out an old newspaper.

"Here's the newspaper that tells all about it," he said, handing it to me. I read the two-column spread, and then I handed the paper to Dick. Dick read it and shook his head.

"Let's go see that fellow," Dick said. "Do you think we have time?"

"We can always take time," I replied.

"I hope you can do something for that boy," Mr. Page said as Dick and I were leaving.

"We'll do whatever we can," I said, "and the Lord will do the rest. And we'll tell Craig that you sent us. He'll be grateful for your concern."

"Let's go back to my house," Dick said as we pulled out of the Page driveway. "I'll ask Bev to hold dinner, and while we're there we can phone the jail to see if they'll let us in."

It only took Dick a few minutes to make the arrangements with the officer at the county jail. He walked into the kitchen where I was talking with Bonnie and Beverly.

177

"It's all set. Let's go."

"Dick," I said as we set out for the jail, "let's pray that the Lord will save Craig."

"All right," Dick agreed.

"Jesus," I prayed, "we're going to see Craig now, as we feel this is Your will. Please save him. Give us the right words to say to him. And please send Your Holy Spirit ahead of us. Amen."

"Amen," Dick added.

We arrived at the jail, and the personnel were very pleasant and helpful. They told us it would only be a minute until we could see Craig. As we waited we both continued to pray silently for him, again asking the Lord to send the Holy Spirit to speak to him before we did.

The deputy motioned for us to come to the steel door. He pushed a button that opened it. We stepped in and were escorted to an elevator which took us to the third floor.

"You will have only about fifteen minutes," he said. "We'll be feeding supper then."

Only fifteen minutes.

"Lord, You're going to have to work fast!" I said silently.

He led us to another steel door and unlocked it for us. It opened into a small room that was bare except for two chairs.

"I'll fetch Craig for you," the deputy said. "And by the way, for whatever it's worth to you, Craig is a fine kid, a model prisoner. Everybody's on his side. It was just one of those things." He left us, saying again, "Just one of those things."

We were praying for Craig when he walked in. He did not look like the man I had first pictured. He looked like just a nice kid who was scared, miserable, and uncertain.

"Can I help you gentlemen?" he asked politely.

We introduced ourselves, and I asked Craig to sit down.

"We're both preachers, Craig, and I'm an ex-con," I explained. "We were visiting with the Pages today, and Mr. Page told us about you and how concerned he was about you. We promised him we would come and see you."

"Mr. Page is a nice man," Craig said. His voice was so low I could hardly hear him. Then he turned to me suddenly, his young face twisted in torment. There was anguish in his voice as he said, "You know, I killed my son. I killed my own son."

My heart went out to him more than to any other person I had ever met. He was only twenty-one years old, and he was so heartbroken and so sad.

"Craig," I said, "there is One Person who can take away all your sorrow. Jesus will forgive you for what you've done, and He can change your life."

"What do you mean?" he asked.

"I'm talking about Jesus Christ. He will forgive you for all the sins you have ever committed. He can make you a brand-new person."

"I go to church," he said meekly.

"It takes more than that," Dick said. "Craig, let me read you some scripture that may explain it a little." Dick read to Craig from 1 Corinthians, 6:9-11:

Know ye not that the unrighteous shall not inherit the kindgom of God? Be not deceived: neither fornicators, nor idolaters, nor adulterers, nor effeminate, nor abusers of themselves with mankind, nor thieves, nor covetous, nor drunkards, nor revilers, nor extortioners shall inherit the kingdom of God. And such were some of you: but ye are washed, but ye are sanctified, but ye are justified in the name of the Lord Jesus, and by the

Spirit of our God.

Dick then explained to him what it meant to be saved and that he too could have this experience.

Craig sat listening, staring at the floor. Tears began to run down his cheeks.

"I killed my son," he said softly. "I killed my son. I killed my son."

"Craig," I asked gently, "why don't you let Jesus take over your life? Ask Him to forgive you. Will you do that?"

"Yes," he replied, his voice barely audible.

I could feel the sweet presence of the Holy Spirit filling the room as I began to pray: "Lord Jesus, you know all about Craig. You know what he's done, and yet You love him. I ask You to forgive him of his sins, even the sin of killing his son. Lord, we realize that You can set him free right here, in the middle of this jail."

Craig, his head bowed low, was swaying in his chair and weeping softly.

"Lord," he said, "I know I'm a terrible sinner. Please forgive me! I'm sorry for killing my son. God, You know how sorry I am! Please forgive me! Please come into my heart!"

As we heard the guard approaching, Craig lifted his head and pulled himself to his feet, wiping his eyes with the back of his hand.

"Now listen to me, Craig," I said, looking at him intently. "We both know you're going to spend time in prison. I'm not going to paint a rosy picture for you. It's a rough place. *But You've got Jesus Christ now, and that makes all the difference in the world.* You trust Him! And don't give up, no matter what."

"Thanks," Craig said. "And thanks for coming."

The guard opened the door, and Craig left us. Dick and I walked out to the car, praising God for once again working where there had seemed to be no hope.

"And thank You for letting me help!" I said. The circumstances were tragic, but joy was welling up inside me.

Chapter
20

Tomorrow and Beyond

After one of our visits to Jackson Prison, Wes and I made arrangements to go on to Lansing to take part in a street meeting conducted by some Lansing Christians. We arrived in Lansing about 9:30 that evening, and as I eased into a parking space, I noticed several kids standing around talking.

"There's our congregation," Wes said, nodding at the group.

"I hope they'll listen," I said doubtfully. I had not had much experience as a street preacher.

"They'll listen," Wes assured me.

We left the car and went into a nearby restaurant, Wes explaining to me that it would be a little while before all the kids were there.

"How many usually show up?" I asked.

"There are usually at least fifty," he said.

"Wow!" I said and turned to look out the window at the kids under the streetlight. My heart was beginning to pound. I was anxious to preach to them, but we sat there for awhile, talking and sipping coffee from worn mugs that didn't look very clean.

At last, just as we were finishing the coffee, a couple of cars pulled up to the curb outside the window and the Lansing leaders of the street meetings scrambled out, laughing and obviously eager.

As Wes and I joined them, one of the young girls climbed up onto the hood of one of the cars and began singing and playing a tambourine. Kids suddenly began to appear from all directions. We realized that some of them were coming to ridicule, but we were thankful to have them anyway.

I was talking with a teen-age girl who was wearing tattered bluejeans, an old maroon sweat shirt and dangling earrings four inches long, when Wes motioned to me.

"It's your turn," he said. "Get up there and preach."

I climbed onto the hood of the car, praying that it wouldn't cave in under me, and opened up my Bible to John 3:16, *"For God so loved the world, that he gave his only begotten Son, that whosoever believeth in him should not perish, but have everlasting life."*

Then I began to talk to the kids from my heart. For the first time, I realized that practically every sermon I preached in my church was designed to motivate sleeping Christians. Here were kids who knew nothing about God. Some of them had never been to church before. Some did not know anything about Jesus, except that He had something to do with Christmas.

A few of the kids were antagonistic.

"Why don't you go away and leave us alone?" a boy shouted.

"Because we love you," I replied. "We want you to meet Jesus Christ."

I talked for awhile longer and then got down and let Wes preach.

While Wes was preaching, a teen-age boy came up to me. His long hair stood out in all directions, and he was wearing a vest made out of wooly stuff that was supposed to look like fur.

"Hey, Man, can I see your Bible a minute?" he said.

"Sure," I said, handing it to him. I thought maybe he wanted to look up John 3:16 and read it for himself. Instead, he walked over to several of his buddies and opened my Bible.

"Look at this dude here!" he laughed, pointing to one of the illustrations in the book. I wondered if they were making fun of John the Baptist dressed in his camel hide!

"Jesus," I prayed silently, "what do I do now?"

Suddenly the boy took my Bible and threw it on the ground, stomped on it as hard as he could, then ground it under his heel.

"Give me that Bible!" I said furiously.

"What's the matter, Man? Don't you like what I did?"

"No," I said. "I don't like it at all!"

"What ya gonna do about it, Man?"

His buddies were encouraging him.

"That's tellin' him, Gary!"

"You tell him, Man!"

"You show these _____ they can't come down here messin' around with us!"

I knew I could get into serious trouble, for some of the kids were obviously high on drugs. They would do anything if the impulse hit them.

"Jesus," I prayed. "Please show me what to do!"

"Tell him that I love him," the Lord said to my heart.

Gary stood there looking at me, with his foot still on my Bible. A few feet away, several girls sat crosslegged on the sidewalk, passing an infant around from one to another.

184

"Gary," I said, "Jesus loves you. And He loves every one of your buddies."

Gary just looked at me. For a moment I thought he was going to strike out at me. A large crowd had gathered, and Wes was preaching to the whole group. The incident between Gary and me was going unnoticed except by a few of his buddies who were standing and watching.

Suddenly, Gary bent down and picked up the Bible.

"Here, Man," he said, handing it to me. "Sorry."

With that, Gary turned and walked away, and his buddies followed him.

I drove home that night praying that revival would come somehow and that more people would be concerned enough to go out into the streets and tell these kids about Jesus.

A few days later I had just finished supper when the phone rang. It was Bob Hunt, a probation officer from Genesee County, of which Flint was the county seat.

"Larry, I've got a man down here at the jail who is pretty upset. Can you come down and see him?"

"Sure," I said. "I'll be right down."

Lance Shedd had been given six months in the county jail because of a probation violation. Two years prior to this, he had escaped a jail sentence only because he had helped to prosecute two other men. In fact, he had helped significantly in the investigation of a crime ring operating in the Flint area. Lance and his two buddies had tried to extort money from the president of a Jackson insurance agency. The other two men had been sent to prison, and Lance was placed on probation.

When I walked in, Lance was sitting with his face buried in his hands. He looked up as he heard me enter.

"I'm Larry Howland," I said, introducing myself. "I was told that you wanted to see me."

As he spoke, Lance began to cry.

"Yeah, I read about you in the paper."

He was referring to an article that had appeared in the paper a couple of months before about the chaplain program in the county jail.

Sometimes prisoners tried to put on an act, but in my heart I knew that Lance was sincere.

"I've been a con man all my life," he said, "and I'm so tired of it. I think I've tried everything but God. Now I want to try Him."

"If you really mean it, Lance, then it's not hard."

"I do," he sobbed. "I do mean it."

I explained to him that he had to pray and ask God to forgive him for his sins and accept Jesus Christ as his Savior and Lord.

"Can I do that now?" Lance asked.

I nodded, and Lance began to pray.

"Oh, God," he cried in anguish, "please, please forgive me for my sins. I know I have done some terrible things, and I'm so sorry for every single one of them. Please forgive me! Lord Jesus Christ, please save me, *please*!"

I had never seen a man who seemed more sincere than Lance was at that moment. Before leaving him, I gave him a Bible and told him to read it and pray. Within the next few weeks he read the New Testament all the way through, plus several other books that I gave him to read. He walked around praising God, and I knew that here was a man who had made a decision to serve God and really meant it. I only wished that the average Christian would get some of Lance's enthusiasm! I rejoiced because of the way he was maturing as a Christian.

As I drove home after one of my visits with Lance, I thought back to San Quentin Prison, and to Jackson Prison and to the Lapeer County Jail. They seemed so far

186

away because my memories of robberies and burglaries were now being crowded out by thoughts of teen-agers and convicts finding Jesus Christ as their Savior.

The house was dark as I pulled into the driveway. Bonnie was in bed asleep. I said my prayers, and as I got into bed I wondered what tomorrow would hold. Serving God was the most exciting thing that had ever happened in my life. Before my conversion, I had dreaded the coming of each new day. Now I looked forward to each one eagerly, not knowing what God would have for me to do next.

I know from my own experience that God *can* change lives in these last days. The Son of God came to seek and to save the lost—whether it was a blind man on the Jericho Road or a self-right-Saul on the Damascus Road. I have a fervent conviction that the same Lord Jesus who walked the Jericho Road two thousand years ago is still alive and working today. Today, in this twentieth century, Jesus Christ can take an ex-convict, or a drug addict, an alcoholic, a prostitute—or anyone in any state of depravity—and restore him and set him free.

I lay in bed that night feeling humbled and awed that a mighty God would reach down into San Quentin Prison, or into the cities of America, into the houses of immorality, into gambling casinos, into skid row, and set free from sin men and women who had done nothing to deserve God's grace.

As I drifted off to sleep, the memories of San Quentin were slowly fading, and the thought of tomorrow and beyond made waking up the next day something very exciting.

"Lord Jesus, I love You!" I whispered. And then I fell asleep.

Inquiries for speaking engagements
should be directed to:

Larry O. Howland
P. O. Box 363
Elsie, Michigan 48831

**WHEREVER PAPERBACKS ARE SOLD
OR USE THIS COUPON**

504 LAUREL DRIVE, MONROEVILLE, PA 15146

**SEND INSPIRATIONAL BOOKS
LISTED BELOW**

Title   Price   ☐ Send
                                                        Complete
                                                        Catalog

_____   _____

_____   _____

_____   _____

_____   _____

_____   _____

_____   _____

_____   _____

_____   _____

Name _____

Street _____

City _____ State _____ Zip _____

Suggested Inspirational Paperback Books

FACE UP WITH A MIRACLE
by Don Basham $1.25

This is a fascinating book about God the Holy Spirit bringing a new dimension into the lives of twentieth-century Christians. It is filled with experiences that testify to a God of miracles being unleashed in our lives right now.

BAPTISM IN THE HOLY SPIRIT: COMMAND OR OPTION?
by Bob Campbell $1.25

A teaching summary on the Holy Spirit, covering the three kinds of baptisms, the various workings of the Holy Spirit, the question of tongues and how to know when you have received the Baptism of the Spirit.

A SCRIPTURAL OUTLINE OF THE BAPTISM   60c
IN THE HOLY SPIRIT by George and Harriet Gillies

Here is a very brief and simple outline of the Baptism in the Holy Spirit, with numerous references under each point. This handy little booklet is a good reference for any question you might have concerning this subject.

A HANDBOOK ON HOLY SPIRIT BAPTISM
by Don Basham $1.25

Questions and answers on the Baptism in the Holy Spirit and speaking in tongues. The book is in great demand, and answers many important questions from within the contemporary Christian Church.

HE SPOKE, AND I WAS STRENGTHENED
by Dick Mills $1.25

An easy-to-read devotional of 52 prophetic scripturally-based messages directed to the businessman, the perfectionist, the bereaved, the lonely, the ambitious and many more.

SEVEN TIMES AROUND
by Bob and Ruth McKee $1.25

A Christian growth story of a family who receives the Baptism in the Holy Spirit and then applies this new experience to solve the family's distressing, but frequently humorous problems.

LET GO!
by Fenelon
95c

Jesus promised a life full of joy and peace. Why then are so many Christians struggling to attain the qualities that Christ said belonged to the child of God? Fenelon speaks firmly—but lovingly to those whose lives have been an uphill battle. Don't miss this one.

VISIONS BEYOND THE VEIL
by H. A. Baker
$1.25

Beggar children who heard the Gospel at a rescue mission in China, received a powerful visitation of the Holy Spirit, during which they saw visions of Heaven and Christ which cannot be explained away. A new revised edition.

DEAR DAD, THIS IS TO ANNOUNCE MY DEATH
by Ric Kast
$1.25

The story of how rock music, drugs and alcohol lead a youth to commit suicide. While Ric waits out the last moments of life, Jesus Christ rescues him from death and gives him a new life.

GATEWAY TO POWER
by Wesley Smith
$1.25

From the boredom of day after day routine and lonely nights of meaningless activity, Wes Smith was caught up into a life of miracles. Dramatic healings, remarkable financial assistance, and exciting escapes from dangerous situations have become part of his life.

SIGI AND I
by Gwen Schmidt
$1.25

The intriguing narration of how two women smuggled Bibles and supplies to Christians behind the Iron Curtain. An impressive account of their simple faith in following the Holy Spirit.

SPIRITUAL POWER
by Don Basham
$1.25

Over 100 received new spiritual power after hearing the author give this important message. The book deals with such topics as the Baptism as a second experience, the primary evidence of the Baptism, and tongues and the "chronic seeker."

THE LAST CHAPTER
by A. W. Rasmussen
$1.45

An absorbing narrative based on the author's own experience, in the charismatic renewal around the world. He presents many fresh insights on fasting, church discipline and Christ's Second Coming.

A HANDBOOK ON TONGUES, INTERPRETATION
AND PROPHECY by Don Basham
$1.25

The second of Don Basham's Handbook series. Again set up in the convenient question and answer format, the book addresses itself to further questions on the Holy Spirit, especially the vocal gifts.